Cascades

General Editor: Geoff Fox

Gregory's Girl

Titles in the *Cascades* series include:

Gregory's Girl

Gerald Cole
Based on a screenplay by
Bill Forsyth

COLLINS EDUCATIONAL

© W.H. Allen and Co Ltd 1981

ISBN 0 00 330012 9

5 6 7 8 9 10

First published by W.H. Allen and Co Ltd, 1981
Published in *Cascades* in 1983 by Collins Educational

Printed in Great Britain by Martins of Berwick

Chapter 1

Gregory Underwood was happy.

It wasn't the fulfilled man's quiet feeling that all is well with the world. It wasn't the sudden benediction granted by a moment of great triumph or unexpected good news. It was sudden, yes, unexpected – certainly – but it came from nowhere. A surge from the subconscious, a brilliance of heart and brain. He glowed.

It was happening to him quite a lot these days.

His father put it down to hormones. Not that Mr Underwood – a quiet, gingery man who taught nervous housewives to drive – had any special insight into his son's mental condition. He simply observed – generally over the breakfast table – that his firstborn, in this, his seventeenth year, had grown five inches closer to the kitchen ceiling. That kind of bodily stretching was bound to stretch the mind as well. Gregory agreed. He stopped on a patch of scrubbed sward, tilting his long, lean, faintly melancholic face toward the sun. The sun was very warm. Sounds of shouting and the thudding of busy feet impinged only faintly on his consciousness. He contemplated his new state.

Perhaps romance was the answer. Not that Gregory felt romantic about anyone in particular – at least anyone he stood a chance of getting to know. It was more the fact that he could, if the opportunity arose. The impulse hung in the air – vague, tremulous, unsullied by the demands of genuine experience. He wouldn't actually object to experience – as long as it was of the right kind. Nothing sordid – not too sordid, anyway. No, his soul craved something finer, something more exalted, something as enthralling as . . . football. His first love. As if on cue, something hard and leathery leapt out of the sun and smacked him fiercely on the forehead.

'Good header! Follow it up!'

Stunned, Gregory lurched sideways. A swarm of panting, purple-faced youths jostled past him. A football boot rasped his ankle.

'Watch yourself!'

'Underwood! Underwood!'

He turned as the swarm panted on. A spare, grim-faced man in a dark blue tracksuit beckoned from the touchline. Gregory raised questioning eyebrows.

'When I made you a striker,' the man hissed in a stage-whisper, 'I didn't mean you had to go on strike.' He glanced suspiciously from side to side, unwilling to share his reprimand with the world at large.

Gregory smiled, as though in appreciation of the little joke. It was a smile calculated to infuriate. It wasn't that Gregory took any vindictive pleasure in being infuriating. It was simply that Philip J. Menzies, gym master of Climackton Comprehensive and team coach of its ill-fated First Eleven, proved such a willing target. In fact, Gregory quite liked him.

Raising an affirmative thumb, Gregory turned back to the game. The rest of the Climackton team were clumped en masse about their own goal, an increasingly familiar sight since the beginning of the game one hour and thirty-eight minutes earlier.

Unexpectedly they gained possession. Gregory's fellow striker – a short, spindly boy called Jeevons – leapt athletically across the goalmouth.

'To me! Back to me!' he yelled.

The ball cannoned from a cluster of mad tackling, striking Jeevons full in the chest. Its force seemed to lift him bodily. Glassy-eyed, he tumbled flat on his back. The ball ambled over his shoulder and past his head as the opposing sweeper bore down, swinging his foot. 'Oh God!' The fallen player closed his eyes. The sweeper missed Jeevons by inches, thumping the ball well into Gregory's half. Mud gently fell on the recumbent Jeevons.

'Flip!' mouthed the Climackton goalkeeper. He was a small, squirrel-faced youth with jug ears and unruly brown hair. He crouched for the onslaught.

6

The whistle blew. The ball smacked past the goalie's outstretched fingers and bounced in the back of the net.

'No goal! Past the whistle! Past the whistle!' he shrieked, leaping up and down.

The opposition striker blew a raspberry at him and performed a cartwheel, jumping up beside his team-mates and shaking jubilant fists in the air. Laughing and cheering, they ran off the field. Gregory, who had just reached the penalty box, paused, breathing heavily, as the Climacktonians shuffled dejectedly past him.

Mumbling, the goalkeeper retrieved the ball from the back of the net. 'Six bloomin' nil,' he snapped. '*Six* bloomin' nil!'

Abruptly Gregory's happiness found its target. It wasn't unruly hormones, it wasn't the spontaneous enjoyment of a noble sport. It was the sheer unbridled absurdity of the last hour and a half. The utter lunacy of total, unmitigated incompetence.

Laughter bubbled involuntarily into his throat. Passing him, Andy the goalkeeper flashed a look of dire warning. As he did so, the ball trickled through his arms, evaded his sudden grasp and darted away between the legs of two crestfallen backs.

Hilarity hit Gregory with the force of mild hysteria. He roared, he doubled up; tears winked in the corners of his eyes. 'Oh –' Andy scrabbled about on the turf – 'get stuffed, Gregory!'

The boys' changing room was long and narrow, its peg-adorned walls rendered mildly offensive by the custard-coloured paint with which the entire school was decorated. Under the strip lighting, the air was heavy with the odours of youthful sweat, steaming showers and ripe feet. Gregory found it oddly comforting. He shrugged on his lurid blue sweat shirt with the Marilyn Monroe print, adjusted his neckchain beneath it and drilled his armpits with a stick deodorant. Then he began to rummage in his holdall for his earring.

He was last to change and now found himself alone. Laughter and running feet echoed down a distant corridor.

7

The showers rumbled asthmatically. School had finished over half an hour ago.

He wondered what to do with the evening. *Top of the Pops* at seven-twenty, of course. After that he might try that new bar near the motorway where Andy had got away with three pints of McEwans the night before. If a baby-face like him could manage it, Gregory should have no trouble.

Then the thought of Andy revived memories of the game and his face creased into a grin.

A foot slapped on the rubber flooring behind him. Pulling on his grey school shirt, he turned. Phil Menzies hung in the doorway, a look of glum uncertainty on his taut, bony face. He seemed surprised, and not at all pleased to find Gregory still here.

Gregory broke the silence with a nodding smile. 'Terrible game, eh?'

The coach's reaction was bizarre. His thin-lipped mouth cracked open fractionally and smoke curled out at either end; his nostrils smoked too. Gregory had a sudden mental image of the man belching flames of demoniac wrath. Then he noticed the half-smoked cigarette cupped in his hand.

Phil stepped into the room, shaking his head and sucking in breath. 'Very bad, very, very bad,' he sighed.

Unabashed, Gregory began to button his shirt. 'You've got to laugh,' he said.

Phil's response was a look of belligerent outrage. The fact that Gregory topped him by some two inches lessened its impact.

'So you think all that was amusing, do you? That farce out there!'

'Oh absolutely,' Greogory agreed, bending for his tie. 'It was laughable. I was thinking we might get booked as a comedy turn. You know, before the big match. Like clowns.' He looked up and caught an expression of wounded horror on the teacher's face. Conscience pricked him. He tried to make amends. 'Football is about enter-tainment, after all. We give them all a good laugh. It's only a game.'

8

Something in Phil's face told him the effort had been wasted. Phil's eyes became stony. 'It's only *eight* games,' he snapped, leaning forward. 'Eight games in a row you've lost.'

Gregory nodded, straightening his tie. 'We can't lose them all. The tide'll turn. You ought to push us really hard, give us lots of discipline. Get tough.'

Phil sighed again, drawing on his cigarette. 'We need *goals*, son. You're not making any goals. That's your job.' He was close under Gregory's chin now; his tone held unusual decision.

Mildly disconcerted, Gregory shrugged. 'Nobody's perfect. It's been a very tricky time for me. I've shot up this year. Can you imagine waking up and finding your legs have sprouted an extra three or four inches? It puts all your co-ordination out.' He crouched down, bringing his face level with Phil's. 'I was very good last year when I was this high.'

He had intended to inject a note of levity, anything to lift this impending gloom. But he had never been this close to Phil's face before, and it suddenly absorbed him. At this distance it looked small and foxy, and a lot older. Gregory wondered exactly how old Phil was. He had always assumed he was reasonably young – which was why he was so easy to talk to. Then he realised why the word 'foxy' had leapt into his mind. 'Are you growing a moustache?' he asked.

Thrown by this unexpected scrutiny, Phil decided not to interrupt his train of thought. 'I want to make some changes,' he declared.

'Good idea.' Gregory smiled and straightened. 'It'll make you look older, though.'

'The team.' Phil blinked slowly. 'I meant changes in the team.' Gregory nodded agreeably and began stuffing his holdall. 'Switch some players around you mean?'

'I was thinking of taking some people out.' Phil was staring hard at Gregory now. 'I was thinking of taking you out.'

'You don't want to do that.'

9

This response was so sudden it surprised both of them. There was a moment of tension.

'Yes I do,' said Phil.

'No you don't.'

'I do.'

'You don't.'

They were staring at each other now, each amazed and slightly appalled at the verbal ping-pong. It seemed right to neither of them. Phil had expected complaints, but not blank defiance. Gregory had simply said the first thing that popped into his head – and was beginning to wonder if he shouldn't have kept quiet.

'Now look –' Phil began – '*Hell's teeth!*' He jumped a foot backwards, flicking away the neglected cigarette which had just burned down to his fingers and showering hot sparks over Gegory's holdall.

The accident dissolved the tension. Magnanimously Gregory let Phil dowse the sparks.

Red-faced, the teacher stepped back. 'I'm thinking very seriously about it,' he said gruffly.

'But why me?' Gregory asked.

'You said yourself,' Phil snapped. 'You're going through a tricky time. You could do with a rest.'

He hadn't been looking at Gregory as he spoke, much more the uncertain and manageable Phil of old. But this unusual note of concern was suddenly disturbing.

'No, what I meant,' said Gregory quickly, 'is that I'm nearly *finished* growing. Another couple of inches and that'll be that. Everything'll snap into place. I'll be fine.'

Phil gazed doubtfully into the distance.

'What about Andy?' said Gregory, suddenly inspired. 'He's hardly *started* growing yet. That's where your trouble's going to be.'

Phil's grunt was non-committal.

Gregory smiled. 'I'll tell him –'

'*I'll* tell him.' Waking up, Phil stabbed a finger at Gregory's chest. 'You're in goal – for a trial period of three weeks. That's what I'm telling Andy and that's what I'm telling *you*!'

10

'Have you got a jersey my size? Andy's much smaller than me.'

'Don't you worry about jerseys.' Phil's look was scathing. 'Three weeks in goal and then I'm going to make a *final* decision.'

'You're the boss,' said Gregory happily. 'Any idea who's getting my position?'

'I want to find some new people.'

The note of impending doom intended to ring through this remark made no obvious impression on Gregory. He shrugged on his dark school blazer, brushed ash ostentatiously off his holdall and snatched the handles. 'You made the right decision,' he said, making for the door and nodding enthusiastically. 'You won't regret this.'

Everything in Phil's steady gaze suggested the opposite.

Chapter 2

Climackton New Town sprawled along the north-facing slope of a long, low, once pine-clad hill. This ensured a constant, though often mild breeze which ruffled Gregory's hair as he stepped off the single decker bus at the stop before the motorway roundabout. The neat redbrick ranks of the Westfield housing estate marched above him. To the left was the old town, a cramped cottage hamlet, all but isolated now with only the old living there and the odd trendy commuter from Glasgow. In the open country beyond, curling into view like a blue ribbon of cigarette smoke, was the motorway. Its low murmur rose from below the roundabout; it was invisible from the bus stop.

Gregory paused at the roadside as the bus drew away. A gaggle of mums and kiddies and a dozen youthful factory workers crossed into the estate behind him. He watched them go and felt suddenly depressed.

There was slightly more reason for it than the euphoria on the football field, but Gregory wasn't convinced. Arguments with Phil Menzies – otherwise known as the Human Dynamo – were common enough. Even the prospect of being thrown out of the First Eleven didn't particularly alarm him. In fact nothing particularly alarmed him these days. That was the most alarming fact of all. He slung his holdall over his shoulder and ambled towards the roundabout. Action, that was what his life lacked. Action with football, action with women, action anywhere! Perhaps he should go, dump school, dump CSEs, get into the real world.

A loud splash interrupted his thoughts. He was drawing level with the west-going motorway sliproad. A large blue sign reared above the grassy curve of the verge. It said GLASGOW 20 MILES. Soapy water was trickling down it.

As he watched, a heavy mop on the end of a long pole

slapped against the sign and began to rub it with a strange rhythm. Slap-slap, pause, slap-slap, pause, slap-slap, slap-slap, slap-slap . . .

Intrigued, Gregory moved onto the roundabout. Now he could see further down the sliproad. Six, no seven figures in fluorescent red safety waistcoats were at work on the slip road verges, sweeping the gutters clean and snipping at the grass. They were very young and very busy, but their waistcoats made them look like animated garden gnomes.

Over the motorway hum, a whistling note caught on the breeze. Gregory paused in recognition. *Snow White and the Seven Dwarfs*! He grinned. Elaborate harmonies developed in the tune, but the gnomes maintained a highly efficient pace.

Of course. He hadn't come here by accident. It was an omen. Teamwork, pulling your weight, that was what adulthood was about. Finding your niche.

He felt better already. To celebrate the moment, he pirouetted, aimed a phantom football at the unseen, easy-going fast lane below and kicked it perfectly. A speeding articulated lorry swerved to avoid it, ploughing through a coachload of Celtic supporters and colliding head-on with a tanker full of North Sea oil, which exploded spectacularly. As the fireball broiled above the roundabout bridge, two more heavy lorries crashed into the concrete supports, causing the entire structure to collapse. In ten seconds it was all over.

Gregory, untroubled by this imaginary apocalypse, suddenly caught sight of Gary.

A solitary, denimed figure was hunched over the parapet of the motorway bridge, halfway across, staring intently at the traffic below. As Gregory saw him, he turned and scribbled something in a note book resting on the parapet beside him.

'Gary!' Gregory called.

The figure glanced up quickly, waved uncertainly and went back to his task. There was something flat and black in his hand which absorbed his attention.

Gregory approached with interest. A muscular, slightly

13

Italianate youth, Gary was Gregory's age but looked much older. He had left Climackton Comprehensive two terms previously. He'd been a confident, masterful pupil, very conscious of his success with women, declaring himself 'too energetic for exams'.

'Car spotting?' said Gregory.

Gary flashed him a swift, sour look. His thumb squeezed the flat rectangle in his palm. It clicked and numbers changed on a digital display. 'Government work. How're you doing in that old dump?'

'Fine.' Gregory manoeuvred to get a closer look at the instrument. 'So you're working then?'

Gary nodded authoritatively, focusing on the motorway. 'Traffic flow data. I'm involved in the daily update. I'm an ennumerator, field operative. It's essential work.'

He spoke it as if reading it off a Job Centre brochure. Gregory recalled he'd never been overly impressed by Gary's intellectual capacity. On the other hand, employment was employment, contributing to the common weal . . .

'Fascinating thingummy jig.' Gregory leaned closer over Gary's right hand. A convoy of Italian fruit lorries thundered past below. Gary's brow furrowed; his thumb clicked furiously.

'What's the money like?'

The motorway cleared momentarily. Gary looked up. 'Not bad . . . not top money, of course.' He smiled for the first time. 'I wish I got paid by the vehicle count. I can log up to fifteen hundred trucks a day here!'

Gregory grunted. The thought of spending an entire day watching the traffic go by didn't sound wildly appealing. 'You just add them up?' he asked.

'No!' The suggestion seemed to strike Gary as a sign of stupendous naivety. 'It's a division as well. Private vehicles, goods vehicles, different nationalities. Then there's hourly totals –' He paused to click off two passing trucks and scribbled in his notebook. 'It's very important to get it right, now I've got responsibilities –' The sentence hung, clearly demanding elucidation. But Gregory had moved back to the counting device, oblivious to the bait.

'I suppose you've heard.' Gary straightened. 'I'm getting married.'

Gregory stared at him. He blinked. Then he laughed. 'You're joking.'

Gary shook his head solemnly. 'No word of a lie. We're having a baby. You know, Fiona and me.'

Gregory's mouth opened slowly. 'My God!' he whispered. His mind was suddenly blank.

'Absolutely,' said Gary.

Gregory turned to the motorway and back again.

'When did it . . . all start?'

Gary sniffed and slipped a hand into his pocket. 'Do you remember that pyjama party at Gordon's place? Round about Easter? When the neighbours called the police in?'

Gregory nodded emphatically.

Gary glanced at the parapet and sniffed again. 'Well it was then.'

Gregory's eyes widened. He was still nodding.

'Or,' said Gary, 'it could have been the night before . . .'

Gregory stopped nodding; the images were multiplying in his brain.

' . . . Or the night after,' Gary finished. He turned to face Gregory's stunned expression. 'It's a marvellous thing, love . . . I hope you're being a good boy, Gregory.'

'Good boy?' Gregory looked at him as if sleep-walking. Then he woke, annoyed to find himself reddening. 'Oh yes, all the time –' He felt suddenly ridiculous, and his face still burned. 'Well –' He swung his holdall, began to back away. 'Keep in touch. I expect I'll see you around. Are you –' his voice threatened to rise an octave and he coughed '– are you staying in town?'

'We're down for a house in Eastfield.' There was a loud rush of vehicles beneath and Gary snatched up his notebook. 'Damn! Did you see that? Was that a Belgian or a French truck?'

'Sorry.' Gregory gestured inanely. 'Didn't catch it. See you.'

'Right. Damn! That's going to ruin my totals . . .' Gary, absorbed in his world of traffic flow, responsibility and fatherhood, was hunched once more over the parapet, counter clicking with Geiger-like speed.

My God!

Feet thudding on the pavement, head lowered, Gregory pounded up the road to Westfield, past the slip-road, past the gnomes. Married. And a father. Gary, the big shot, lording it over the fourth form; Gregory had half expected him to duck exams, he'd even felt – go on, get it out – superior! Bloody superior! Now Gary had done it again, right out of the blue, pipped everyone at the post. A father. He'd done it that many times!

Gregory sighed loudly. And with Fiona. A little blonde bombshell with a face sweet as sin and . . . He swallowed hard at the memory.

He remembered that party. His first promised orgy, except that all the girls seemed to have sewn their nighties to their underwear; most of the ones he'd met were wearing more than they did at school. One pecked kiss he'd had, one begrudged peck from a semi-inebriated giggler. While Gary – perhaps in the bedroom upstairs – or even in the same room! It took an effort not to bite on his knuckle.

He swung into his close, striding now. Well that was it. Altruism, teamwork was all very well, but the common weal could roll just as well without him. Now was a time for individual effort, individual achievement. He *had* to get a woman. Or, he considered, tired now as he went through his front gate, it was time to be doing something very decisive about it.

Under the glare of the full moon, the hooded lights flanking the twisting asphalted path looked like fairylight decorations. The path climbed the side of a low, grassy hill; to the right dim fields sloped away towards the flickering lights of the motorway; to the left a belt of trees, intermixed with dense undergrowth, smothered the hill crest. The undergrowth squeezed untidily through the horizontal bars of a wooden waist-high fence.

Gregory paused in his upward climb, glanced swiftly behind him and straddled the path. He bunched his knees, bent his arms at the elbows and clenched his fists so that his knuckles faced forward. Then he contorted his face into a look of insensate ferocity, baring his teeth and making his eyes pop. Pumping arms and legs up and down in an identical rhythm, but leaving his torso rigid, he began to shuffle across the width of the path, still facing forward, and making loud pinging and whistling noises.

When he reached the motorway side of the path, he leapt forward two feet, his posture unchanged, and began to shuffle back, pinging and whistling again. This activity masked the approach of a small cloaked figure. It was a bustling middle-aged nurse, arms folded protectively inside her cape, who appeared round a bend in the path, descending the hill. Flapping past on flat heels, she cast a swift, suspicious stare at Gregory who blushed fiercely, coughed and shook his arms experimentally as if throwing off a sudden violent cramp.

'Gordon Bennett,' he mouthed, wincing and hopping sideways. The nurse threw him a further, wilder look before vanishing around a lower bend. Gregory was nervous and even Space Invader imitations weren't going to improve his state of mind. He was wearing faded blue jeans, scuffed green training shoes and a grey Levi sweat shirt decorated with stains, but his armpits were still sticky; his palms itched. It was a balmy night. He was only here, he reminded himself, because Andy was out when he called – supposedly visiting Eric the camera freak – and Eric, when he called, had also been out, which left the pub or the country park – both of which had proved to be Andy and Eric-less – or here. He thought of sneaking a quick glance round the bend where the nurse had disappeared, and decided against it. If his nervous gestures hadn't already aroused the suspicions of any potential observers, he wasn't going out of his way to confirm them. Sniffing, he wandered towards the wood-side fence, leaned against it nonchalantly as if sampling the evening air, sniffed again and then vaulted over the top.

The well-trod tunnel through the undergrowth had a damp earthy smell. Leaves flicked against his face. He

17

moved quickly and quietly, bent almost double, stretching a protective hand in front of him though there was ample light filtering down from the searchlight moon. His face assumed its Clint Eastwood mask, frozen immobility, the imminence of violent action.

Ahead the undergrowth was thinning. A light appeared through the leaves, high up, then another, then a row.

A voice hissed distinctly: 'Where is it? I can't see.'

Gregory froze, balancing on the balls of his feet. The voice seemed only a few feet away in the dimness. He hadn't heard enough to recognise it. After an age leaves rustled.

A deeper voice whispered: 'In the middle ... there ... *there*!'

'Yeah, I've got it ... I've got it ...'

It was Andy, the rapt tone was unmistakable.

A third, slightly hoarse voice, chimed in: 'She's getting undressed ... my God, she's down to her slip ...'

This proved too much for Gregory. Lurching forward, he snagged a branch on the edge of his sweatshirt. An entire bush at his side seemed to leap suddenly a foot to the right. Four startled youths shot to their feet from a shadowy depression in the undergrowth just in front of him.

'*Damn it, Gregory!*'

It was Eric, gruff and bespectacled, the moon silvering his glasses. Behind him, faces pale and staring, were Andy, his quiet friend Charlie, and Pete, another First Eleven veteran, reputed to be a world champion cultivator of acne.

'Sorry,' said Gregory, sinking back into the darkness with them.

'She's back ... she's back ...' hissed Andy.

Instantly all five concentrated on the scene before them. They were huddled at the end of a crescent-shaped lawn at the rear of a long, two-story building. Most of the rooms on the ground floor were dark, except for one where part of a blackboard and an upright human skeleton were visible. On the first floor four or five rooms showed lights, but only one had the curtains open.

Framed there in profile, well lit from below by what

18

appeared to be a dressing-table light, stood a young woman, pensively biting a full lip as she unpicked a nurse's cap from her hair. Her hair was dark and short-cropped, her face round and lively and her figure full beneath a plain white slip.

'Oh please,' rasped Andy. 'Please make it come off . . . please God, make it come off . . .'

Gregory swallowed. He could feel sweat breaking out all over his body.

'Concentrate,' ordered Eric. 'Use telepathy. Tell her to take it off. Altogether, transmit!'

'Take it off . . . please, Miss . . . take it off!' murmured Andy.

The woman put some pins into her mouth, glanced back into the room and lowered her head, tensing slightly in concentration.

Andy's murmur deepened into a druidic drone. 'You will take off your slip . . . you *want* to take off your slip . . . your slip is hot and clinging . . . you will take it off . . .'

'Concentrate!' hissed Eric. 'You're not trying – transmit!'

Abruptly, oblivious to this telepathic barrage, the nurse turned and vanished inside.

'She's gone, where's she gone?' gabbled Pete.

'Calm down,' whispered Eric. 'She's in the wardrobe.'

'Oh, come back, please come back . . .' Andy's hands clasped together.

The curtain shifted slightly; the nurse, capless now, rose from the window ledge, evidently having deposited something beneath. It was a fraction of a second before the upward light caught her slim, bared shoulders.

'Oh blimey . . .!'

'A bra!'

'Look at that!'

Her head was down; she was folding something, each movement setting shadows dancing across her pale skin.

' . . . Three seconds, four seconds . . .' counted Pete.

Andy, his hands grinding together, began to rock on his feet. 'I can't believe it . . . I can't breathe . . . I can't see right . . .'

So bizarre was his tone the others were forced to glance at him.

'Come on, Andy . . . grow up!' Gregory growled.

'Six seconds, *seven seconds*!' gasped Pete.

Shivering violently, Andy staggered sideways. 'I can't see right . . . I'm going to faint . . .'

His protestations were so loud now there was a real chance of discovery. His arms were grasped by Eric and Gregory; dragging him, they edged back into the undergrowth, eyes still fixed on the window. There the nurse lifted her head and half turned into the room. Closing her eyes, she gently massaged the nape of her neck. The profile presented was breath-taking.

'Wow, Eric,' Pete whispered, hobbling as he tried to walk backwards.

'Where's your camera? What a picture!'

'I know . . . I know,' Eric breathed, nodding and letting Andy sink slowly into the foliage at his side. 'You could make a fortune with a picture like that.'

'What a doll!' Andy's ecstatic sigh rose from a patch of leafy darkness. 'What an absolute doll!'

A feathery leaf caressed Gregory's chin. His heart was thundering and his knees felt uncertain. He wanted to jump about and scream to stop himself shaking uncontrollably. To know a girl like that. Sweet, sweet delirium . . .

Yawning, the nurse snapped her eyes open and walked across the room, disappearing from their view.

'Twelve seconds,' whispered Pete. '*Twelve* whole seconds. That's a record.'

Andy struggled to his feet. 'We'll come back tomorrow, eh? Make a night of it. I'll bring sandwiches.'

Gregory looked round the circle of pale, bright-eyed faces.

'Fantastic,' he breathed. 'Absolutely fantastic.'

Shaking their heads in disbelief, all five faded back into the undergrowth. For a moment only the soft swishing of branches marked their passage, followed by silence.

Then, from a point barely a dozen feet from where the others had crouched, two crop-haired youngsters, no more than ten years old, rose into view wearing expressions of sophisticated disdain.

'What a lot of fuss over a girl's bra,' said the first scornfully. His companion nodded, chewing casually on a mouthful of gum.

'You're not wrong.' He paused, distracted by a sudden movement in the window above them. 'Hey look – she's taking it off . . .'

Chapter 3

Gregory woke.

Daylight was slanting through the open curtains with the orange floral pattern and splashing across a new Partick Thistle team poster hanging opposite the door. He blinked twice, for a wild moment uncertain who or where he was.

He sat up. A pale, tousle-haired visage leered bleary-eyed at him from the wardrobe mirror at the foot of the bed.

Yes, of course.

Reassured, he sighed and sank back onto the rumpled pillow. Drawn curtains meant that his mother had already been in to call him – a fact he dimly remembered; he'd simply dozed off again, which he always did, because he was tired and hated getting up early and because his dozing dreams were invariably more vivid and impressive than the usual kind. Dreams like the dark-haired nurse in the window appearing inexplicably at his side during a typically disastrous First Eleven game. He'd been aware of her legs first – an important omission from his activities of the night before – long, slim, tanned a light coffee, they matched his stride for stride. He was pleased about that. Next he'd been aware of her face, sharper featured than he remembered with a longer nose and darker skin, but so real he had begun to wonder if she wasn't somebody else. She'd been smiling, a broad, brilliant Cheshire cat smile, directed at him constantly regardless of the fact they were supposed to be racing hell for leather down a busy football pitch.

He gave a long, strangulated groan, halfway to a whimper, and stopped suddenly, aware that he might be heard outside. A milk float rattled to a halt in the close beyond the window. The house seemed quiet. He breathed out slowly. An uneasy thought popped into the forefront of his mind. Hadn't his mother mentioned something about taking Madeleine his ten-year-old sister to the dentist this morning, leaving early? It explained the silence below. His father would have left first as usual. Wincing, Gregory snatched his black digital watch off the bedside table. Ten past nine.

School roll call had been at ten to, assembly at nine; the first period would begin in ten minutes. He could infiltrate the second, borrow Madeleine's dental appointment as an excuse.

This was the second time this week and it was only Tuesday. Vaulting out of bed, he decided that it wasn't being late itself that was so annoying, it was being found out, the inconvenience of having to explain a perfectly ordinary human failing like sleeping too long. Or – to be honest – sleeping as long as he needed to function at maximum efficiency. After all, what was the point of arriving on time only to slump over your desk? Throwing off his pyjama top, he resolved to build on that as his second line of defence in case the dentist began to look shaky. With any luck he'd run into the Human Dynamo first. Phil would appreciate an argument like that. He grinned, and then noticed the uncurtained window. He shrugged his top back on, crossed the room and closed the curtains.

He hated to be overlooked when he was dressing.

Gregory stared in the bathroom mirror, hooded his eyes and pouted his lips, letting the lower one hang loosely. He sniffed, dissatisfied, and rumpled his unkempt hair into a mass of spiky points. He looked again, closer, and experimented with letting his lower lip droop even further. Gradually his whole face twisted into a parody of ape-like rage. 'Ah hayut Tayuesdays!' he snarled, thrusting forward the hand that held his soap-sodden flannel. Two spots appeared on the glass and began to trickle downwards. He hunched one shoulder and growled louder: 'Ayum goana shoot thuh whoal day down!' Satisfied, he reviewed his phrasing in his memory. His expression resumed its usual bland melancholia. There was no doubt about it. He was looking more like Bob Geldof every day.

While the percolator his father had threatened to repair for all of a month coughed and wheezed in irregular spasms on the sink top, Gregory scraped some breakfast together. Strictly speaking he should have forgotten food, but he'd only snatched a snack the night before and he was feeling the pangs.

On balance cereal seemed too much bother, particularly as Madeleine had scoffed the last of the ReadyBrek. Rifling the fridge, he found some well-preserved baked beans in a plastic box and scooped them out with a forgotten crust of stale white bread. He had a passion for stale crusts. Finishing the beans before the crust, he smeared it liberally with Marmite and lemon curd. Visually it looked interesting but the taste was questionable.

By this time the percolator had subsided into grumbling inactivity. He poured out a thin, luke-warm liquid that was greyish in colour. He decided to make do with a half bottle of ginger ale in the back of the fridge.

On the way out he scooped a wedge of shortcake out of the biscuit tin. There was a half-eaten Wagonwheel inside rewrapped with loving care. Momentarily he agonised over this, but he knew the Wagonwheel was Madeleine's; he wouldn't touch it; they had an agreement about that sort of thing. Instead he took another two wedges of shortcake and munched them along the hallway.

From the hallstand by the front door he lifted his blazer, shrugged it on and found his briefcase – which was in fact a battered satchel from which the shoulder strap had been forcibly removed – in a clutter of boots and shoes below.

He took a final look at himself in the hall mirror opposite. He sighed, squeezed the satchel under his arm and used his free hand to pull his blazer collar upright. After a few seconds' consideration, he loosened his tie and undid the top button of his shirt.

He screwed up his face speculatively. Something was missing. The penny dropped; he must have been asleep.

Slipping two fingers into his blazer's breast pocket he fished out his earring, put down his satchel and clipped it in, mouthing 'Ouch' silently. He ought to go back to the little shop in the precinct and get a re-bore, but he was reluctant, having been followed in last time by a gaggle of giggling teenyboppers who had taken him less than seriously.

Still . . . He took a final final look at himself. Considering that he wasn't God's gift to the women of Climackton, he didn't look too bad. Obviously studenty, but not untrendy.

He wondered idly if he ought to have tried shaving again. It had been three days since the last attempt and the wounds had just about healed. Then he remembered the time.

The sun beamed down on traffic-free Dumfries Close, glinting off the shiny slate roofs of the houses opposite, the new grey plastic guttering beneath them and the white road sign where the 'D' in 'Dumfries' had been skilfully transformed into an 'B'.

Pre-school squeals filled the clear air. A phalanx of toddlers on trikes thundered past Gregory, shrieking wildly, and forcing him off the pavement. At the corner a cherub-faced little girl in a crisp lemon dress was straddling an even smaller boy in a red anorak, pummelling his chest; his eyes were closed and he was giggling.

'Hello Gregory,' said the little girl, looking up as he passed.

'Hello Gregory,' said the victim, opening his eyes and squinting in the sun.

'Hello Mary, hello Jeremy,' said Gregory, hurrying on.

'I'm *Timmy*!' the little boy yelled with great force.

'Sorry,' said Gregory.

'*Hello Gregory*!' The voice came from a tree in the middle of an adjoining garden. Perched on a narrow branch that was plainly too frail to support her was a three-year-old girl with black frothy hair. It was a second before Gregory spotted the sturdy plum-coloured supporting post beneath the branch, though he couldn't imagine how she could have made the climb unaided. She seemed to be playing imitating games.

'Hello Gregory! Hello Gregory! Gregory! Gregory!'

Taking up the general cry, the wild trikers had wheeled across the close and were thundering back towards him.

Kids, he thought, not unkindly, and turned into St Mungo's Way. He didn't mind them at this age. After all he was still half a kid himself. And they didn't have to worry about impressing the opposite sex. The point about that, he considered, negotiating Glencoe Passage, skirting the top

25

of Culloden Close and entering Flodden Way which led down to the motorway roundabout and the bus stop, was the injustice of it – especially for blokes.

It was all very well looking out for 'a mature and stable adult relationship', as a red-faced Miss Welch had advocated in Civics recently – but not when most mature and stable adults regarded you as a spotty infant, or when the only girls you knew worth serious sexual consideration were obsessed with older men of at least eighteen, who could offer maturity, mobility and a lot more spending money than Gregory.

By way of a confidence booster he executed a perfect forward pass, and watched Kenny Dalglish slap it into goal. He continued down Flodden Way as Scotland's answer to Glen Hoddle, returning to his jubilant but otherwise humble home after an amazing World Cup victory.

There was a queue of young mothers with infants in collapsible push-chairs at the bus stop. The last woman turned to glance at him. He stopped swaggering.

No, biology was the catch. It simply didn't allow any time for maturity, stability or adulthood. Not when your pores started imitating Mount Vesuvius and a half glance from a pretty girl could bring you down with terminal blushing.

A young mother in a plastic raincoat joined the queue just before him. There was a baby strapped papoose-style to her front in a harness that left its rubbery legs free. It burped at him companionably over the mother's shoulder, and began to dribble. Hence the plastic mack, Gregory thought absently, wrinkling his nose. And that of course was the end result of mature and stable adulthood. Domesticity and Farley's Rusks and dribble marks down the wallpaper.

Like Gary and Fiona.

To be honest he couldn't violently object. It meant independence and money and a woman waiting at home every night. Even if it was the same woman. He wouldn't even mind that terribly.

He shuffled his feet, aware that constantly thinking about sex only made it worse. Didn't he have enough to worry about? Wasn't he hanging onto the First Eleven by a thread, by one ragged football lace . . . ? And never mind CSEs . . . He straightened with sudden resolution. Then the single decker bus nosed into view a hundred yards up the road and he remembered why he'd bothered to wait for it when school was only twenty minutes' walk away.

Her face was a rounded triangle with high cheekbones and large, soft, bluish eyes, widely spaced. Her hair, bunched at her shoulders, was a silvery blonde, scalloped backwards in long, sweeping curls that danced at every movement. Her lips, equal and perfect bows, pouting only slightly, curved in a subtle and unforced smile that lit up her entire face. With the softest exhalation of breath they parted, moved liquidly over white even teeth. She spoke: 'All aboard ladies. Right money if you please. Move down inside.'

Phantom violinists played arpeggios up and down Gregory's spine. In his eagerness to give up his fare, to make contact, he bounded onto the upper step of the bus entrance, jostling the papoose mother and the woman in front of her who was bending to collapse a baby chair. The papoose baby hiccuped at him. The bending mother flashed an angry look at the papoose woman, who, constricted by her baby, tried vainly to turn. Gregory gazed at the lady bus driver.

His stomach trembled in rhythm with the bus's shuddering diesel. He felt light-headed; he found difficulty breathing. She was beautiful. There was no doubt of that. Not just in the perfect symmetry of her face, the way her light-grey uniform traced her trim bosom, the firm but feminine manner in which her slim fingers gripped the gear change, but in herself. Her attitude; her smile, especially directed at him.

The papoose mother moved aside with a peeved look she had saved up. Gregory confronted the blonde angel. She smiled at him; he beamed back, pressing his face forward, wondering if the contact of hands might bring sparks.

'Thirteen,' he said hoarsely. He dropped the coins into her palm.

'There's only twelve here, pet,' she said.

27

Panicking, crimson to his black creased moccasins, he rummaged in his trouser pocket, grinning stupidly, almost tumbling his satchel onto her lap. 'Yes of course. Absolutely right... Haven't woken up yet... Absolutely ...' He sounded absurdly pompous, middle-aged.

He found a fivepence piece, pushed it into her hand and was forcing his two pence piece back into his trouser pocket before he realised she was waiting to give him a further two pence change. 'Ah... yes...'

Taking it, juggling again with his satchel, he caught her smile. Brilliant, subtly knowing. She saw right through him; she understood every wicked impulse. Electricity re-established. Reassured, beaming again, he moved down the bus, tripped against the wheel of a collapsed baby chair and dropped into the first empty seat.

The bus stopped shuddering and eased away up Flodden Way. It was easy being a man of the world, Gregory considered, sweating only slightly now. Chatting with beautiful women, passing the time of day, both of you realising and relishing the sexual attraction and yet, because you were both otherwise engaged, business to be attended to, deciding to let it hang for the moment. Everything in due time.

He settled himself down, pushed his ticket into his breast pocket and smiled companionably at the woman sitting next to him. It was the papoose mother, her baby gurgling softly on her lap. Both ignored him.

The bus turned right up Methven Hill Rise, and began to climb. There were houses on one side, trees on the other. In a few seconds the trees gave way to a plain redbrick Victorian building with a dusty asphalt forecourt. A sign read: ST AGNES' NURSES' ANNEX. The bus squealed to a halt just beyond it.

Gregory strained forward, anxious to catch the driver's profile. A flock of black-caped nurses squeezed through the opening doors, chatting and laughing, and clustered round the driver's seat. Annoyed that his view was obscured, Gregory leaned into the aisle. The first nurse broke away down the bus, turning her head and chuckling as she came. She had short, brunette hair, a round face, lively eyes.

28

Gregory froze. For a brief moment he hadn't recognised her with her uniform on. She looked exactly the same as in his dreams, except her eyes were a little watery and her nose reddened from a cold obviously caused by wandering around semi-nude in front of draughty windows. He was hideously, mind-sappingly embarrassed.

Reaching him, the girl caught his blatant, crimson-faced stare. She gave him an odd, disconcerted look, lowered her head and passed. She was much younger than he'd realised, hardly out of her teens, only two or three years older than himself. Somehow that made it far worse.

The other nurses began to move down the bus. He adjusted the satchel on his lap, coughed quietly and glanced ostentatiously out of the window. All this stimulation so early in the day was doing him no good. He'd be a nervous wreck by the time he arrived at school and totally incapable of lying through his teeth.

At the next stop – the one before Climackton Comprehensive – he made his escape, regretting his cowardice the moment his foot touched the pavement. He watched the bus draw away, then, remembering the time again, hurried off across some open ground.

Mr Underwood's Hush-Puppied foot hovered uneasily over the dual control footbrake as he wondered, for the second time that morning, if he was sharing his driving school car with a maniac. In the ten years he'd been an instructor the prospect had often loomed, though never quite materialised, which surely meant the likelihood of it was increasing all the time. After all Climackton had a population of 50,000 plus, and, according to statistics, one in every hundred people suffered from some kind of mental disorder during their lives; that meant at least 500 prospective berserkers wandering the streets – or driving down them. Always remembering, of course, that two hundred and fifty of those five hundred – not to mention twenty-five of those fifty thousand – would be women, which to Mr Underwood's mind made them a little strange to begin with.

At least he couldn't accuse Mr Clark of being a woman.

'Turn right here,' he said, as the Escort crawled slowly over the crest of Methven Hill Rise, the grey roof of the nurses' hostel rising through the trees on their left. He took the opportunity to study his pupil more closely.

Mr Clark was a narrow, bony man, with a narrow bony face, flat jet black hair, even darker spectacles and a complexion that suggested he had lived most of his life under a large stone. He wore a patched tweed jacket, a buttoned woolly cardigan beneath it and shiny suit trousers. He sat hunched forward in the driving seat, his long bony fingers gripping the top of the wheel with *rigor mortis*-like tenacity, his small sunken eyes fixed on the road ahead. There was an air of faintly malicious intensity about him. He looked like an unsuccessful embezzler, newly released from prison and about to wreak a terrible revenge on society, or possibly a district council clerk who had worked in the rent arrears department and had just been made redundant, which as it happened, was exactly what he was.

'Right,' he echoed bitterly. 'Turn right.'

'Mirror and indicator,' intoned Mr Underwood. 'As soon as it's clear, move to the crown of the road.'

Fortunately the road was entirely empty. Even though the Escort had not topped twenty-five miles an hour since leaving the school premises, he had the distinct feeling that the sight of one vulnerable pedestrian would inflame his pupil, prompting a sudden murderous surge forward.

'Gentle pressure on the brake and down to second,' he said, dismissing the thought. There really wasn't any point in growing paranoid. It was totally unprofessional – and out of character. Mr Underwood was a wry, placid man who enjoyed comfortable armchairs, an evening pipe and the occasional humiliation of Celtic. His unnatural nervousness had to be caused by parental worry; the staggering normality of young Madeleine – and Gregory. Gregory who'd arrived home late last night covered in leafmould and grass stains and insisting everything was fine. Or so Ruthie had said, because he had missed number one son himself by shutting his eyes for thirty seconds during the Closedown. With any normal youth he'd suspect him of breaking and entering or despoiling telephone kiosks, but with a youth as quixotic as Gregory anything was possible.

'Nicely done,' he told Mr Clark, as the car eased round the turn at a gentle running pace and began to move off slowly beside a patch of treeless green.

'Up into third now and a little more accelerator.'

'Accelerator,' said his pupil, as if insulted; his forward gaze was unwavering.

'The advantages of learning how to drive in a new town environment, of course,' said Mr Underwod, 'are the absence of traffic lights – just a touch more accelerator – and the total absence of stray pedestrians.' He risked a brief sidelong glance to see if the key word had brought any response. It hadn't. 'But you must remember,' he continued, 'that in other towns things won't be anything like so controlled...'

He paused. The road, so reassuringly empty a moment ago, was now occupied. Some fifty yards away from where the green ended in a tarpaulined pile of builders' materials, a lean, darkly dressed, oddly familiar figure had stepped out into the roadway, and was beginning to lope briskly down it away from them.

A mesmeric moment followed.

The car crawled towards the figure at a steady fifteen miles an hour. The figure, having apparently abandoned all thought of crossing, acknowledged the vehicle's pursuit with a half turn of the head and simply quickened his pace down the middle of the road. Mr Clark, riveted to the steering wheel, gave no sign that he had noticed anything untoward.

Imminent disaster suddenly stared Mr Underwood in the face. 'Mirror and brake!' he snapped, Hush Puppies dropping to the floor. 'I have control. That's it...'

Mr Clark's only response was a faint hiss of released breath through compressed lips. He seemed disappointed. The rogue pedestrian, only yards ahead, made absent-minded sallies to left and right, then resumed the centre path.

'Relaxed driving position,' Mr Underwood encouraged, touching the wheel and nudging the vehicle leftward around the figure. Obligingly, it too veered to the left.

31

'Brake!' cried Mr Underwood, stamping hard. The car jolted to a halt and stalled, the pedestrian's hand slapping on the bonnet – but only to steady himself, not as a reproof.

In fact he still barely admitted the car's existence, glancing blandly from left to right, his gaze skipping over it as though it were some minor unimportant blot on the landscape. Doing this, he finally appeared to spot the far side of the road, and began to lope towards it.

Mr Underwood wound down his window. 'Come here you!'

Gregory turned in surprise, as though addressed from thin air. His expression lightened as he faced the car for the first time.

'Was that an emergency stop?' accused Mr Clark.

'Yes,' replied Mr Underwood absently, 'Unsimulated . . .'

Gregory appeared at his window, smiling brightly. 'Hi, Mike!'

'Shouldn't you have rapped the dashboard? I thought that was normal procedure,' persisted Mr Clark.

'Not when unsimulated,' Mr Underwood hurried. He turned back to the window, lowering his voice. 'Call me "dad", Gregory, or "pop", or something. It makes me feel better when you call me "dad".'

Gregory nodded with a bland smile; he ducked his head towards Mr Clark. 'Listen, I won't take up your time . . . I know you have to concentrate when you're under instruction . . . I'll leave you to it.'

Mr Clark, still gripping the wheel, returned a basilisk stare.

With another smiling nod, Gregory backed away.

'Stay Gregory!' His father's tone checked him. 'I'm sure,' said Mr Underwood more calmly, 'Mr Clark would like a minute or two to collect his thoughts . . .' The pupil snorted loudly. 'What's the score anyway? Are you going to school late or going home early?'

Gregory paused, his gaze wandering. It was, reflected Mr Underwood, going to be another of those non-conversations that seemed to characterise his entire verbal com-

32

munication with his teenage offspring. Direct questions from Mr Underwood, startling non-sequiturs from Gregory. He'd often toyed with the idea of suggesting some private, more neutral language, like Esperanto or Urdu, as an aid to clearer communication. It certainly couldn't make their conversation any less intelligible.

Gregory smiled warmly. 'How are you anyway?' he asked, his parrying skill clearly not up to scratch at this hour of the day.

'Fine,' replied Mr Underwood politely. 'We're all very well. Your mother was asking about you only the other day. I told her we had met in the hallway briefly last Thursday and you looked fine . . .' Delivered with only the faintest touch of sarcasm, the words plainly had an effect on Gregory; his smile grew lop-sided. 'Listen, I've got an idea,' Mr Underwood persevered. 'Why don't we meet up for breakfast some time later this week . . . say eight o'clock in the kitchen, Friday? Your mother would like that . . .'

Out-manoeuvred, Gregory was obliged to treat the invitation seriously. 'Yes . . .' he offered uncertainly, then brightened. 'That sounds fine . . . yes.'

Mr Underwood, heartened by this rare victory, allowed himself a smile. 'It's a date then.'

He turned to the driving seat. 'Ignition, mirror, signal, gear, Mr Clark.'

Snorting, the pupil brought the car back to life.

'And we'll start some driving lessons as soon as you've mastered the walking on the pavement bit . . . OK?' Mr Underwood beamed at his son.

Gregory smiled wanly.

The car lurched away, leaving him standing. What a very *nice* day, thought Mr Underwood, watching his son stride off in the mirror.

'I'll expect extra instruction for delays,' growled Mr Clark.

The window-sill of Climackton Comprehensive's first floor staffroom was painted a bright orange in livid contrast to the custard colour of the walls. It was also thick with dust.

33

Alec Wilson, senior biology master, drew a slender, disapproving finger along it, sniffed and wiped the digit clean on the underside of his saucer. 'Every blasted morning,' he announced. He was a tall, pale-faced man with a passion for scarlet waistcoats; he was wearing one now.

Bending to a plate containing sponge cakes on a small table beside him, Alistair Stewart raised a quizzical eyebrow. Then he realised Alec was now gazing out of the window. He picked up some sponge and leaned over the table to look. The window provided an excellent view of the boys' playground at the front of the school. The main gate was directly ahead; to the left were the cycle sheds, to the right a row of Portakabins housing the woodwork and metalwork shops. Gregory, who had just entered the playground obliquely and at great speed, was now strolling with an exaggerated nonchalance along the side of the Portakabins. Reaching a side door, he stopped, bent to tie a shoelace then abruptly made a bee-line for the cycle sheds.

'He's mad,' commented Alistair. 'He should be locked up.' He munched dourly at his sponge cake, and seemed surprised at its quality. Short and bespectacled with a permanent five o'clock shadow, he was a history teacher who had just begun teaching religion in order to rise a grade. He enjoyed the extra money but the subject depressed him immensely. The two men were alone in the staffroom, enjoying a rare free period.

As they continued to watch Gregory's progress, Phil Menzies padded past in the corridor outside, spotted the tea cups through the open door and hovered, expectantly.

'Any tea?' he asked.

'He must think he's invisible,' Alistair continued, ignoring him.

Alec snorted. 'Stupid idiot.'

Uncertainty clouded Phil's face. Used as he was to insult, it seemed unlikely that his colleagues would be quite so blatant. He entered the room, noting with chagrin that the electric kettle in the sink in the corner was unplugged. He could only spare two minutes. 'Who is it?' he asked, reaching the window. Simultaneously, Gregory, who had been approaching the main entrance under cover of the cycle sheds, vanished from view.

'He's gone now,' said Alec, turning away. 'It was that daft boy in the fifth year. He's in your football team. I heard they were awarded a corner last week and did a lap of honour.' He exchanged a scathing smile with Alistair, and sipped at his tea.

Phil, who had just realised who they meant, frowned worriedly. 'Oh him. His days are numbered. Next week he's out! Kaput... finished.' He nodded darkly. 'I'm getting some new blood into the team, making some big changes...'

'Have a sponge cake Phil,' said Alistair.

'... A new regime, starting right now,' Phil continued. He nodded again, accepting a cake. 'In fact I'm signing a new striker this very morning. Then you'll see...' He paused, looking at the cake with deep suspicion. 'Who made these?' he asked.

'Relax,' said Alec urbanely. 'It was Alice and Sandra in 3A. Very nice girls... very clean.'

An uncharacteristic grin creased Phil's spare features. 'Oh aye... Alice and Sandra, is it? Very nice girls, eh Alec? Do you still get the wee poems from June as well eh?' He made to nudge Alec's elbow, winking obliquely at Alistair.

Alec veered away, shielding his tea cup.

'You'll get put away!' Phil grinned. He chuckled and munched his cake noisily, obviously pleased with the note of rough male banter he had introduced.

Alistair, unmoved by the outburst, suddenly narrowed his eyes and stared at Phil closely. 'I like your moustache,' he said.

Phil swallowed hard and nodded. 'Does it show already? I've only been growing it a day or so. Thanks a lot.'

'You'll look more grown-up,' Alec commented drily.

Phil seemed pleased. 'Do you think so?'

Alistair squinted at him over his tea cup. 'Very mature.'

'Yes,' said Alec. 'You look at least fifteen already.'

The pleasure drained abruptly from Phil's face; he reddened slightly. There was a pause. Then he rubbed his hands. 'Well, I've got to scram. Pretty important morning. I've got some new players to put through their paces. One place in the team for the best striker. I've organised a contest . . . see what they're like under pressure . . .' He was burbling and he knew it. His colleagues regarded him coolly, giving no help. He retreated, still slightly pink, to the door. 'Well . . . see you later.' He coughed and vanished.

Alec and Alistair looked at each other and smiled faintly. Alec drained his cup and took it to the corner top.

Alistair went to the window table and picked up another cake. Just as he was about to take a bite, he paused. '*Are* you still getting the poems from June?' he asked.

Chapter 4

Phil Menzies loped away from the staffroom, limbs swinging purposefully, eyes raking the after-break corridor like an eager forward sweeper. He looked decisive – so decisive, in fact, that a dawdling first-former, wandering inadvertently into his field of vision, swerved guiltily aside.

The movement heartened Phil. He didn't feel decisive at all. At least not in the way he suspected eager forward sweepers felt. His feelings approximated more to an extremely thin, slightly brittle *wafer* of determination.

This emotional wafer was sandwiched between an unshakeable faith in the redeeming powers of Football – hopefully to be manifested through the school's First Eleven – and an equally deep, and rather better founded suspicion that Somebody Up There had it in for him. It was the closest he ever came to real certainty. In future, he promised himself, he would stop confiding his plans to the staffroom. Professional jealousy was a terrible thing.

Results, that was what counted finally. Results would stop the scoffers. One good new striker, a little application, slightly more luck than of late – overnight the world could be transformed. Momentarily he indulged in a brief flash of fantasy. Cheering crowds as the rejuvenated First Eleven smashed its way to the top of the Climackton Junior League; newspaper headlines as eight team members were selected for the Strathclyde Under-Sixteens; two members in the Scottish Schoolboys: 'I owe it all to the basic grounding I received at the hands of Philip J. Menzies,' claims . . .

Then he turned the corner towards the gym and saw Gregory.

Earring sparkling, neck chain glistening in the bleak strip lighting, Gregory slouched towards him with that look of artless benignity that both disturbed and infuriated Phil. It wasn't that Gregory was particularly obnoxious; he rarely

37

picked his nose in public and he didn't make rude noises in the showers like that revolting McVicar boy (surely that wasn't all nerves?). No, Underwood's misdemeanours were more subtle. Like calling football 'only a game'. Phil shuddered at the memory. Or convulsing a gym class by quoting a perfectly reasonable passage from a sports report: 'Dalglish dribbled the length of the field then picked his spot.' 'Well what else would you expect him to do?' Phil had enquired angrily, setting off a fresh adolescent fit. Phil distrusted subtlety, unless it involved a neat tactic or a tricky piece of footwork.

Cursing under his breath, he glanced round swiftly for an exit. The corridor was empty in both directions. He couldn't pretend to miss the boy. Sucking in breath, Phil decided to brazen it out. Accelerating to near jogging speed, he steered towards his tormentor, head tucked into his shoulders. At the last minute he straightened up. 'Might have some news for you by lunchtime, son,' he snapped off briskly. 'Keep you posted. All right?'

He didn't wait for the reply. Congratulating himself on having neatly sidestepped an awkward situation, he breezed round the next corner and vanished in the direction of the gym.

Gregory stared after him blankly. Having successfully slipped into school, he had found to his annoyance that he had missed the start of the second period by minutes. He had debated whether to brazen out a late appearance or simply wait and quietly infiltrate the third. Five minutes' serious cogitation had led him several miles away – on the bus route into school where a demented Scots Nat. terrorist had hijacked the bus, forcing Gregory to leap to the rescue of the blonde driver with only a baby carriage and a Farley's rusk to hand. Unsurprisingly he hadn't noticed Phil at all until he'd spoken. Now he was intrigued. Had the Human Dynamo had a change of heart? Postponing his heroic daydream for a more suitable moment, he reversed direction and set off in Phil's footsteps. Half a dozen First Eleven hopefuls clustered around the goal mouth on playing field number one, the closest to the gym entrance.

It was a bright, clear morning. High clouds scudded overhead. Seagulls imitated confetti on the further pitches. Emerging from the gym with a wobbling string-bag of footballs, Phil was pleasantly surprised. After the first team's latest results, he had been prepared for no more than two or three diehards to answer his noticeboard advertisement.

True, only one of this crew was showing enough initiative to jog on the spot and work up a little preliminary sweat. And their interpretation of regulation gear was more catholic than he would have preferred; the colours of their shorts – one pair of which dangled at knee height – spanned the spectrum, and one faded blue vest bore the dim but unmistakeable outline of Mickey Mouse. But there was an unexpected sense of anticipation here, a groundswell of genuine enthusiasm. The day was looking up.

'Right!' Padding up to them, he deposited the footballs in the goal mouth and drew the boys round him. 'You all know what I'm looking for,' he began. 'A goal scorer! And that means two things. Ball control, shooting accuracy – and *the ability to read the game!*'

Rapt looks confirmed that he had struck the right note. Only one boy – a small, weasel-faced lad – seemed doubtful.

'Clear?' Phil nodded at him.

'You said two things,' replied the boy. 'Do you mean that ball control and shooting accuracy are aspects of the same thing, as distinct from the ability to read the game, or that shooting acuracy and –'

'What?' Phil glared at him with deep suspicion. Was the Underwood syndrome seeping through the ranks?

The boy was unperturbed. 'You just said there were two things and then you went on –'

Phil's narrowing gaze fell to the boy's shoes. 'You're wearing plimsolls,' he interrupted.

The boy did not even look down. 'It's all right,' he said brightly. 'I'll buy some proper boots if I get into the team –'

'Oh no, son.' Phil shook his head gravely, his expression mellowing. Suddenly he was on safer ground; the image of Underwood receded. 'No, you can't handle the ball

39

properly without the proper footwear. Sorry son. Go and get changed.'

The boy's bland expression slipped; his mouth opened.

Phil turned away, raising his voice. 'We play in the right boots in this team, from the word go. We do things properly here or not at all.' His tone took in the remainder of the hopefuls; a couple swapped smug glances. Latent team spirit, Phil observed with satisfaction. Build on it. Establish who is boss.

The plimsoll-wearer flapped away disconsolately.

'Good!' Phil clapped his hands together, bent to the string-bag and shook the footballs free. 'We'll begin your trial with simple ball control. Remember that's one of the two – three – most important skills you'll need.' There was a brief scramble for the balls. 'I want you to trot with the ball at your feet, fifty yards down the field and back. Two lines. Go!'

Eagerly they burst away from the goal mouth in a bobbing, weaving mass, separated into two ragged lines, bunched, then broke again into two vaguely disparate groups.

'Both sides of the foot!' Phil shouted after them.

The boy in the Mickey Mouse vest trod on his ball, tripped heavily and fell.

'Let me see complete control,' Phil urged.

Mickey Mouse picked himself up, swung at the ball and missed. The others, several yards ahead of him by now, merged once more into a single group.

Alarmed, Mickey Mouse swung again. His foot connected viciously; the ball rocketed through the air and smacked into the neck of the nearest dribbler. An altercation developed.

'Keep moving!' Phil bellowed. 'This is a trial, remember!' Vague murmurs wafted downwind to him. The dribblers dribbled on. Breathing in deeply, Phil rocked back on his heels. I am not going to be disappointed, he told himself. Things are going to be done properly. Despair is *not* in my nature.

It was at this point that things began to go seriously wrong. Much later – through the amber, anaesthetic glow

40

of a third pint – he would review the events of the morning in search of some slight premonition of disaster. Try as he might he could not find one. His ancient BSA had started at first kick, his moustache had sprouted a further full milli- metre – even Alistair and Alec had noticed that – and Sandra McAlpine had almost smiled at him in assembly.

The footballers had reached the mid-field and were start- ing to mill about, obviously in some uncertainty about the fifty-yard limit. Frowning, Phil stepped from the goal mouth, beckoning them back impatiently.

He had been dimly aware of a figure approaching from the school building. Track-suited, with blonde, loose- flowing hair, it registered vaguely as feminine, clearly a messenger from Miss McAlpine's class. The imminence of distraction only added to his growing annoyance. Sensing the girl behind him, he murmured without turning: 'What do you want, lass?'

Before she could reply, he stepped forward again, bawling: 'Get some pace into it! Anyone can *walk* with a ball...' His words had no discernible effect. Sighing, he subsided, aware only then that the girl had made no attempt to answer him. He threw a peeved half glance in her direction. 'Can I help you, dear?'

Cool, china-blue eyes returned a look of icy self-con- tainment. It was a look that demanded attention. Phil recognised it at once, if not the girl. It was the hallmark of the fifth form clique Alec had dubbed – only half-jokingly – as 'gaol-bait 5A'.

Pubescent glamour pusses, incipient Mata Haris, young women blossoming disturbingly in dusty classrooms. Phil, who had troubles enough, normally avoided them like the plague.

'Isn't it, er ...?' A name popped out of his memory. 'Dorothy –'

'I'm here for the trial,' she said simply.

For a moment, too tied up with other thoughts, Phil failed to understand. 'Yes, it's not going too badly. We need a lot more work, of course. Discipline.' He nodded authoritatively, glancing back at the boys. It worried him

41

that the girl's determined stare was not softening. The appalling suspicion entered his mind that his track suit might have split at the back again.

'I saw the notice,' the girl spoke again. 'Football trials. Eleven a.m.'

Slowly, as rampant Sioux on the point of massacre might have heard the distant echo of a US Cavalry bugle, her meaning began to filter through Phil's comprehension. He looked at her uneasily. 'Yes, the boys are doing quite well . . . the lads . . . I'm sure Miss McAlpine is busy with the hockey team, do you know?'

If the girl did, it clearly made little difference to her.

'Look, sweetheart –' Casting a glance at the returning mob, Phil lowered his voice – 'you do realise this is *football*. For the *boys* –'

'Didn't say so on the notice,' she said flatly. 'It just said "talented players".'

Her look was adamantine. Phil accepted it warily, daring the mask to crack. If she was playing some kind of joke . . . He knew, even as he looked, that she was not. He tried a conciliatory laugh. 'I'm sorry you misunderstood, dear. Everyone makes mistakes; there's no shame in that –' He gestured magnanimously, his sweeping arm including the boys who now padded up to the goal-posts and, panting, stood about, gazing with open curiosity from Phil to Dorothy.

'You didn't say "boys only"', Dorothy persisted. 'And anyway you're not allowed to. I want a trial.'

Phil felt a battery of faces bearing down on him, freezing his expression of enforced bonhomie in a look of genuine horror. For a fraction of a second the events of the last few moments flashed in action replay through his mind. How exactly *had* he involved himself in this absurd, embarrassing situation? The internal logic of it all defeated him. By then he had lost the impetus to explode in anger. Instead he simply opened his mouth, forgetting he had not decided what to say. 'No, love, it's just not possible, not at the moment. We don't even have a spare ball. You leave it with me and I'll fix something up with Miss . . .'

Dorothy was moving away from him. She went straight to the ball the weasel-faced plimsoll-wearer had discarded, flicked it effortlessly into the air and balanced it on her palm. She regarded Phil with an air of flinty triumph. 'Here's one.'

Their eyes locked; the challenge was now explicit. Later – on his fourth pint – Phil would decide this was the crucial moment, his final opportunity to nip this feminine usurpation in the bud. At the time he was aware of no such thing. The only thought that flickered through his suddenly blank mind was a bleak premonition that his BSA would never reach home tonight without breaking down at least once.

'Right!' He swung quickly on the assembled boys. 'Let's have some more trotting with the ball, shall we? Two lines again, and I want to see some real speed. Let's get to it!'

With sinking heart, he watched Dorothy streak to the head of a line; her slim limbs pumped with effortless grace; her full lips tightened in total concentration. The ball seemed to be attached to her feet by elastic. She looked back only once, a fierce snatched glance full of undisguised meaning.

Perhaps, thought Phil, it was Alec whom Sandra McAlpine had almost smiled at in assembly; Alec had, after all, been standing directly behind him. The more he thought about it, the more likely it seemed.

Puzzled, Gregory moved away from the shadow of the gym entrance and stepped onto the grass. Though it was his unerring instinct to seek cover whenever he found himself in places he shouldn't be, the events on the football field were proving much too interesting to miss.

At first he'd paid only scant attention to the trim, dark-suited girl who'd moved so purposefully across the field towards Phil – though the way her blonde hair bounced had reminded him momentarily of his bus driver. But as soon as he'd noticed the disconcerting effect she was clearly having on the Human Dynamo, his interest had quickened. Not that disconcerting Phil was any feat. Gregory tended to do it without thinking these days. But an attractive girl added a certain novelty.

And then the girl had picked up the football and moved. Moved like a female Pele, a golden-haired Dalglish, a curvaceous Kevin Keegan. Reaching the touchline, Gregory paused, transfixed. He was aware that something extraordinary was happening – not merely at the far end of the field where the blonde was expertly slamming ball after ball into the net past a befuddled and plainly outclassed defender – but somewhere inside him. Something chemical. Tingling. It was rather like flu.

The world seemed to retreat and sharpen focus all at the same time. Suddenly all five male footballers were ungainly puppets, their strings jerking out of rhythm. The girl weaved between them, weaved, bobbed, danced and shot like a track-suited goddess. Her movements had a natural fluency; she had class, she had style, she had . . .

' . . . Magic,' breathed Gregory.

'That's Dorothy from 5A,' a voice announced at his side.

'Dorothy,' echoed Gregory. He did not turn.

Andy, who'd only wandered over idly to see what Gregory found so absorbing, glanced at him speculatively. He swapped a curious look with Charlie, who, Laurel to his Hardy, hovered silently beside him. 'She's football mad. Worse than some lads.'

If Gregory heard he gave no indication; his expression was rapt.

Out on the field a red-faced Phil Menzies was trying stalwartly to salvage some authority. 'Three shots each at goal!' he cried. Elbowing the last defender aside, he positioned himself between the posts and nodded to Dorothy. 'We're looking for accuracy now . . . Best of three shots . . .'

Dorothy placed the ball, aimed and drew back her foot.

'Don't be shy now –'

The ball cannoned past his left ear.

'What a dream . . .' breathed Gregory. ' . . . What an absolute dream . . .'

Andy and Charlie's eyebrows flashed semaphore messages at each other. This was not the Gregory they knew and loathed.

Dorothy's third shot rocketed past Phil within inches of his stomach. His hands clutched at empty air. He glared at her as the ball bounced in the back of the net. The girl's face was a mask of concentration. Curtly Phil nodded to a waiting boy to shoot.

Gregory was glowing. The inner tingling had risen to his skin. He felt a warm, roseate balm enfolding him. It was much nicer than flu.

'She's got funny ears,' offered Andy.

Mickey Mouse's last ball curved smoothly into Phil's chest. He grasped it gratefully and decided to cut his losses. 'Right boys, that's it ... Just show me some stamina now. Once round the field and back to the dressing rooms. It's only half a mile and should be tackled as a sprint ... On your way.'

They hared off. Phil gathered up the footballs and started towards the school. He looked back only once. At the second corner Dorothy was in the lead and pulling away. Phil sighed uneasily. On the touchline Andy and Charlie became aware that the gym teacher was padding grim-faced towards them. They began to drift away, remembering they should be elsewhere. Gregory did not move. His eyes were fixed on the slim, athletic figure now rounding the third corner of the field. The pack were several yards behind. Dorothy was angling towards the gym entrance, clearly aiming to intercept Phil. Her blonde mop streamed behind her. Gregory's heart began to hammer.

She passed him within a dozen yards. Her face was only moderately flushed, her eyes bright, shining, brimming with purpose. Lightish blue, Gregory noted. His favourite colour. His stare was blatant but Dorothy only had eyes for Phil. She skipped to a halt beside him, hardly breathless.

'Well?' she asked.

Andy and Charlie, who'd wandered off along the touchline, paused and turned to listen. This had all the hallmarks of a confrontation.

Phil was grunting: 'I'll let everyone know in the fullness of time. I'll pass the word to Miss McAlpine.'

Dorothy's face darkened; she manoeuvred in front of him, checking his escape.

'I was the best! You *know* I was the best!'

As if to underline the point the boys stumbled past, purple-faced and panting.

'OK dear.' Phil risked Dorothy's direct gaze. 'You *were* the best. You're good but it's just not that simple. It could be out of my hands. We'll have to see . . .'

Dorothy was implacable. 'If I was the best I should be in the team. The notice said so.'

Phil sighed heavily; his sidelong look, which took in Gregory, was a mute call for help, but Gregory was on a different planet.

'She's a tiger,' he thought. 'She's a goddess. She's eating him alive!'

Phil lowered his head and his tone. 'You might very well get into the team . . . I said we'll see. You could get in . . . We'll work it out soon.' And he bolted, sidestepping her neatly, making for the cover of the gym.

In a flash Dorothy was after him, dogging his footsteps.

'You've got to put me on the team list. I want to sign something. You've got to let me sign something . . .'

The shadow of the gym swallowed them up.

There was a sudden silence. Andy looked wonderingly at Charlie; Charlie looked back. They both took in Gregory. He seemed definitely – odd.

Whatever planet he was on it was not earth. It was much closer to heaven, and his first angel had just wafted by. 'What a dream,' he murmured. Football *and* a figure. His eyes widened at the impossible, perfect vision. 'What an absolute dream . . .'

Chapter 5

Gregory's life had changed. There was no doubt about it. Absolutely none. Great things were upon him.

For the first time his life had meaning. Direction. A path. And it led straight into the clear blue eyes and sweet-smelling hair of Dorothy.

Dorothy. The name had an extraordinary aura all of its own. He wrote it in block capitals next to the death of Caesar in his New Clarendon edition of *Julius Caesar*; he etched it in heavy gothic across the foreword of his Steinbeck's *German Grammar*; he inscribed it in stark computer type on the flyleaf of his Galston's *Basic Geometry*. He even began to biro it on the tiled wall of a cubicle in the boys' lavatory but decided the site was inappropriate and rubbed it out. How had he never noticed her before? How could he have gone through his entire school existence without stumbling over such an image of perfection? Why had he never seen her at work with a football? He was bemused, he was blessed, he would start to walk to school. He wanted to shout his good fortune from the rooftops. He wanted to sit on it quietly for a while in case someone laughed. Within an hour the pressure was enormous. He decided to compromise. He would tell Steve.

'Hands,' ordered Steve.

Gregory, who had been rolling up his sleeves, submitted them dutifully.

'Flip!' snapped a feminine voice across the kitchen. Gregory glanced round. The air was thick was the hiss of steam, the clatter of saucepans, the dull rattle of busy mixing bowls as two dozen CSE cookery students, of varying abilities, slaved over twelve electric cookers with the menu of the day. From the far corner Mrs Lewis, the white-coated cookery teacher, gave him an exasperated look. Gregory smiled deprecatingly.

He was feeling very nervous, and it had little to do with the fact he was six minutes late for the class. Now, he had decided, was the moment he would make his great anounce-ment – or at least launch it tentatively and judge the prevailing wind. He had already tried twice – once during the economic causes of the First World War this morning, and again at lunch. But Steve was a hard man to pin down. He was an entrepreneur, a businessman, a budding Charles Forte. He was also an excellent and painstaking cook.

'Other side,' he said.

Gregory turned his hands over. There was a small brown stain on his left thumbnail. 'That's just paint,' he said hastily.

Steve sucked his teeth in grudging acceptance. He was a dour, fleshy youth with a square, shrewd face. 'OK. I've got the biscuit mix started, you get on with the sponge and put the oven on, 450 degrees.'

'Yes, boss,' Gregory turned enthusiastically to the work surface at his side. Steve – always liable to be touchy in these surroundings – was placated. Gregory could talk to him when the cake mix – or whatever it happened to be – was safely installed in the oven. He snapped open the cupboard doors below the worktop, reached out a large plastic mixing bowl and slapped it on the top, gently nudging Steve, who was already mixing at a speed to put most blenders to shame. 'Sorry,' said Gregory.

Steve, long inured to his partner's culinary ineptitude, nodded slowly. As if to cement his position of supremacy, a pretty girl with straight shiny dark hair chose that moment to appear at his side.

'Steve,' she said, 'can you help me out with this pastry mix thing?' Her apron was awry and she looked confused.

'Hello Susan,' said Gregory, rising.

She gave him a cool glance and turned her attention to Steve, who sighed theatrically and laid down his whisk.

He turned to her slowly, the prophet descending from the mountain. It was plainly a role he enjoyed. 'What kind of pastry? There's more than one, you know. Is it rough puff, short crust, flaky, suet . . .?'

A horrified blankness overtook Susan's face.

Steve took pity. 'Just tell me, what are you making?'

Susan sighed. 'A meat pie. Margaret's doing the strudel soup, and I'm doing the pie. It's the eggs for the pastry I'm not sure about . . .'

This was too much for Steve to resist. A broad smile split his face. 'Strudel soup eh? I'd like to try some of that.' He glanced at the still hovering Gregory, who smiled thinly; he had no idea what Steve was on about but instinctively he had no wish to upset Susan.

'It's *noodle* soup,' Steve declared. 'And what eggs? You don't put eggs in a pastry. It's eight ounces of flour, four ounces of margarine . . .'

' . . . A pinch of salt,' Gregory threw in helpfully.

' . . . Some salt,' Steve continued. 'Mix it all up, into the oven for fifteen minutes, and that's it. OK? No eggs, no strudels, nothing.'

His sarcasm evidently had greater effect on Susan than the advice.

'Is *that* all?' she said, tossing her head. 'That's *simple.*'

As she crossed the classroom, the imprint of Steve's floury hand was just discernible on the back of her neat skirt.

Steve shook his head sagely and resumed his high speed mixing. 'To think there are five guys in the sixth form crying themselves to sleep over her.'

'Six if you count the music teacher,' said Gregory. He broke three large eggs into his bowl, picked out the pieces of shell and spooned in sugar. He found a fork and began to beat the mixture vigorously.

'Watch your mixing,' warned Steve. 'It goes stiff if you overdo it. You only need thirty seconds.' He snapped his fingers. 'Give me the sugar.'

Gregory handed over the packet, which Steve took without looking up. Gregory remembered the oven and bent to turn it on. He glanced at Steve. The oven would take some time to heat and the conversation had already touched on sex. It seemed as good a time as any to make his move. 'It's time *you* were in love, Steve. Take your mind

49

off all this.' His nonchalant emphasis on 'you' he thought quite good; subtle enough to hint at something unspoken without really revealing it openly.

Unfortunately the subtlety seemed to elude Steve. Scraping up a mass of limp dough, he slapped it on the worktop and began to belabour it with a heavy wooden rolling pin. 'Plenty of time for love,' he announced. 'I'm going to be a sex maniac first. Start this summer. Get rid of my apron and let my hair down. Put love potions in my biscuits.' He gave an evil chuckle and thwacked the dough savagely. 'Anyway I want to be rich first, so that I can get off with something really . . .' His eyes glazed momentarily at the prospect '. . . expensive.'

It wasn't quite the level of sympathetic understanding Gregory had anticipated. But he had committed himself. 'You're daft,' he said airily. 'You should try it. Love's great.'

'Who told you?'

'I'm in love.' Absently he stirred the sponge mix with his finger. It was this, more than anything else, that drew Steve's attention.

'Since when?' he said.

'Since this morning,' said Gregory. 'I can't eat. I probably won't sleep a wink tonight. When I think about it I feel dizzy . . .' He sighed, smiling. 'It's wonderful . . .'

'Sounds more like indigestion to me,' said Steve; his eyes were still fixed on the mixing bowl.

'I'm *serious*,' said Gregory, pained.

'Maybe you're pregnant; they put weird things in the toothpaste these days . . .' Steve's frustration got the better of him; snatching Gregory's finger from the mixing bowl, he began to wipe it clean with kitchen roll. Gregory submitted easily, clearly wrapped in dreams of his beloved.

'Come on then – who is it?' snapped Steve, growing impatient; the oven was nearly hot.

'You'll just laugh and tell everybody,' said Gregory shyly.

'Give me a clue,' Steve pleaded.

Gregory looked into the sponge mix; it was beginning to worry him that things were getting so specific.

50

'It's somebody in the football team.'

There was a silence. Steve's dour expression betrayed nothing. Three cookers away Susan let out another disgusted 'Flip!' which was followed by a hiss of scalding pastry mix.

Steve leaned closer to Gregory. 'Have you mentioned this to anyone else? Listen, it's probably just a phase . . . Is it Andy? Is it Pete?'

Gregory stared at him, appalled. 'Come on! I mean Dorothy. She came into the team a couple of days ago. She's in 5A.' Sweet memory melted his outrage. 'She's a wonderful player. She goes round with Carol and Margo. She's got lovely long hair, she always looks really clean and fresh and she smells, mmm . . .' He was grinning now with a kind of helpless idiocy. 'Gorgeous . . . Even if you just pass her in the corridor. And she's got teeth, lovely teeth, lovely white, white teeth . . .'

'Oh *that* Dorothy,' said Steve. 'The hair . . . the smell . . . the teeth. *That* Dorothy.'

With the prospect of startling revelations receding, Steve's interest waned; he went back to his rolling pin.

'That's her, that's Dorothy,' Gregory leaned forward excitedly, planting one hand on the work top, missing it and landing in his mixing bowl instead.

'The one that took your place in the team,' said Steve dourly.

'So what? She's a good footballer.' Gregory considered the remark almost rude; he began to scrape sponge mix off his hand. 'She might be a bit light but she's got skill; she's a fantastic girl . . .'

'Can she cook?' said Steve. 'Can she do this?' He scooped a wafer thin disc of pastry off the worktop and juggled it in the air with a pizza-maker's flourish.

This struck Gregory as unnecessarily flippant. It was beginning to dawn on him that infatuation was likely to be a lonely business.

'When you're in love,' he declared solemnly, 'things like that don't matter.'

'Gimme the margarine,' said Steve.

51

An objective observer might have detected a hint of envy in his tone, but Gregory was too involved in his own state of mind; he needed reassurance. 'Do you think she'll love me back?' he asked tentatively. He handed over the margarine, picked up his fork and began stirring again.

'No chance,' said Steve. 'Watch that mix. I told you, nice and slowly. Take it easy . . .' He took Gregory's hands in his, guiding him through the motions of a correct mixing. Central as it was to Steve's preoccupations, it was still a friendly act. They were, after all, mates.

Gregory tried again. 'What do you mean, no chance?'

Steve sucked his teeth; he would go no further; prolonged discussion could ruin a good baking. 'No chance,' he said flatly.

Gregory looked glum. For the first time unease joined the rather pleasant nervous tingling he felt and he wasn't at all sure if he liked it. At least, he consoled himself, he'd made sure no one else was aware of his predicament.

Chapter 6

'Gregory seems pretty keen on that Dorothy, eh?' Andy commented.

There was a note of enforced cheerfulness in his voice – a determination to make do. It brought very little response from Charlie, a bland, rubbery-lipped youth with a lank, blonde fringe. Andy sniffed, squirming in his chair. Very little ever seemed to bring a response from Charlie. Andy didn't mind; he was sharp enough and talkative enough for both of them. It was something else that was bothering him.

He turned from the tight cluster of chairs where they sat in the corner of the senior common room, and glanced across the room at the source of this discomfort. In the opposite corner, spotlit by a blaze of brilliant sunshine slanting through a picture window, a fifth form girl and boy were entwined on the same plastic chair, lips plastered fiercely together, eyes tight shut. They moved only fractionally, breathing expertly through their noses. They seemed to have been at it for hours.

Glancing away, Andy resumed his line of thought with difficulty: 'Doesn't stand a chance... At least he's trying though...' Behind him the couple's chair squeaked. 'Which is more than we're doing...' A note of exasperation entered Andy's voice. He knew if he had the courage he would go over and complain but he was sure he'd be doing it more out of envy than anything else. He didn't embarrass easily.

A soft giggle reached his ears. It was too much. Andy leaned forward. 'Charlie, we've got to get some girls, we've got to make a move. Even Gregory's at it now. We're falling behind –'

He threw a fierce, desperate look over his shoulder. The lovers, still oblivious to the outside world, seemed unchanged. 'I don't think,' he said quietly, 'there's any advantage in putting it off any longer.'

53

A shrill, banshee-like wail rose from the large square at the back of the main school building. From far off, it sounded like a battlefield of harpies. Close to it became less diffuse; a babble of recognisably human voices, mostly high-pitched, and punctuated by shrieks, squeals and screams of anguish or delight. Pete opened the rear door and advanced with trepidation. There were more than five hundred girls in the girls' playground and he was the only male in sight.

He wandered for a moment before he picked out his target among the bobbing, dark-blazered throng. They stood in a small enclave between the oil storage tank and a low wall guarding the entrance to the boiler room. It was in the farthest corner of the playground. Sighing, Pete entered the crowd. A particulary livid spot had erupted in the centre of his forehead overnight; there was nothing he could do about it and it embarrassed him hideously. He was halfway home before Dorothy caught sight of him.

She dropped the football she was carrying, trapped it under her foot, then flipped it expertly toward Margo. 'We have a visitor,' she said.

Margo caught the ball between foot and ankle, let it fall then drop-kicked it to Liz who dribbled it towards the boiler room wall, twisted and passed it back to Dorothy.

'Oh yes,' said Susan, who was sitting on the wall. 'I do believe I "spot" him.'

Carol, leaning against the brickwork beside her, chuckled sardonically. 'He looks like a walking traffic light,' she said.

Dorothy, once more in control of the ball, dribbled it in a circle, turned and kicked it at waist height toward Pete who by now was only yards away. Caught unawares, he made a vain effort to lift his leg high enough to stop it, changed his mind and smacked the ball awkwardly to the ground, bouncing it several times as if he'd intended that action all along.

The five members of Alec's 'gaol-bait 5A' regarded him coolly.

'Nice ball, Dorothy,' he said, tossing it back to her. 'Very light.'

54

'Nice ball?' Her blue-eyed gaze radiated disdain. 'It's only a Telstar 5, only the best professional football in Europe!'

Even less sure of himself, Pete looked blankly at the ball.

'Does Telstar 5 mean nothing to you?' asked Margo incredulously.

Liz emitted a faint giggle.

'I *said* it was a nice ball,' Pete snapped, reddening. 'Anyway can I borrow it at three? Just for an hour. Andy forgot his.'

Dorothy hugged the ball protectively to her blazer. 'Can you not borrow one from some of the wee boys in the first year?' she asked. 'This is a bit special. It's too good to be belted round a playground.'

Pete, the ground now totally knocked from beneath his feet, retreated into near abject apology. 'I'm sorry. I thought it was just a ball.'

'That's OK.' Dorothy decided to be magnanimous. 'It's not your fault.'

Pete smiled bleakly. Next time he'd listen to his instincts. He knew he shouldn't have made this embarrassing trek. He turned and made a beeline for the safety of the main building. Dorothy dropped the ball and kicked it into the shadow of the wall. She was tired of practice, which meant it was over for the moment. This was her enclave; here she was the prime mover.

'Do you think he's still a virgin?' wondered Liz. She was still looking after after the retreating Pete.

'He can't be,' said Susan, twisting her legs on the wall, her neat page-boy swinging. 'He's been in the school orchestra for over a year.'

'Someone told me you can tell by the way they walk,' said Liz thoughtfully.

All of them turned to look. Pete was sidestepping to avoid two wrestling first formers; he had a long, loping stride.

'Really?' said Dorothy, intrigued.

'Gregory must be then,' said Carol, remembering another prominent loper.

'*Who*?' chimed Margo and Liz together. They all stared at Carol.

55

'That boy in goal now,' she said, her tone suggesting mild idiocy in the questioners. 'Used to play inside right. What do you make of him, Dorothy?'

She considered for a moment. 'He was slow in the forward line, and I think he's too awkward for goal,' she pronounced.

Carol blinked slowly. 'I mean do you *fancy* him. He's crazy for you.' The others moved in closer; this had the air of intrigue.

'Oh?' Dorothy displayed unfeigned disinterest; ever since the 17-year-old paperboy at home had started slipping love notes to her in *The Scotsman* a year and a half ago, she had come to expect a certain amount of male attention.

Susan was swift to corroborate the news. 'I saw him in French yesterday. He couldn't take his eyes off you. He stared at your legs for ages.' There was admiration in her voice: Dorothy had unquestioned glamour. And Gregory – she smiled – Gregory reminded her of a particularly dense ostrich. 'He was even drooling at your schoolbag,' she finished.

Dorothy laughed. 'What a wally!'Her scorn killed the topic. There was a hiatus. The girls let their attention wander about the playground. 'Oh by the way,' said Carol eventually, 'Pete's not a virgin.'

Two nights after falling in love Gregory went into training.

It wasn't a snap decision, he told himself; he'd been planning to increase his fitness for some weeks now; he was, after all, a leading light in the First Eleven.

This was the same reason he gave the Human Dynamo when he encountered him, quite deliberately, outside the gym just after four. Phil, after ignoring Gregory's first call and then remembering two vitally urgent appointments, listened with deep suspicion. Then disbelief. Then even deeper suspicion. 'Apart from anything else,' Gregory continued enthusiastically, 'I was reading that if your body and your muscles are well developed by the time you're eighteen then you stay like that for the rest of your life. I just thought I'd get in early.'

Actually he hadn't read it; Andy had told him over a particularly stodgy plum duff at lunchtime. But the point seemed to have its effect on Phil. The suspicion seeped out of his eyes and he rattled out the details of a regime so punishing it would have made a Canadian airman blanch – appropriately so since he had just read about it in a book of Canadian Air Force exercises Miss McAlpine had lent him that morning. To his surprise, Gregory lapped it up.

'Sounds great,' he enthused. 'Fantastic. That's really it. By the way –' He practically tickled Phil under the chin. 'That moustache is really coming on well!'

Wide-eyed, Phil watched him lope down the corridor, execute two imaginary passes and exit round a corner. He released a silent breath of relief. For a mad moment there he'd been on the point of lending the boy McAlpine's book. A fatal move; the lad was obviously sickening for something – he'd never have got the damn thing back.

Gregory, meanwhile, exulted. He'd re-established his enthusiasm for the game, for the team – for treading the same turf as Dorothy. They'd never throw him out now. Dorothy and Gregory, striker and goalie. Fellow professionals, they'd be unbeatable! He wasn't in training for the First Eleven – he could acknowledge it now, secretly, joyously – he was in training for love.

The ball arched high over the St Mungo half of the field, aiming, it seemed, inexorably for Pete's right foot. Backing towards the opposition goal, he flashed glances from left to right; the two St Mungo backs were racing for him from behind; their midfield players bore down from the right. None could reach him if he was swift.

He judged the ball, he dipped his forehead for the header, tensed and jumped. 'Aagh!' Agony racked him as the ball smacked the still swollen eruption in the middle of his forehead. His boot snagged a tussock of grass. With a final wail, he tumbled backwards, glimpsing through watering eyes the burly St Mungo striker who lifted the ball neatly with his right foot, spun and cleared it.

'Come on!' yelled Dorothy, swerving past. 'Keep up the

57

pressure!' With a fierce flash from china blue eyes, she was gone. Groaning, Pete climbed awkwardly to his feet.

'This is a real farce, a total shambles,' Andy commented bitterly from the far end of the field. 'Eight games lost in a row and what do we do? Sack the goalie and put a girl in the forward line. It's a madhouse . . .' Hunched and tense, he bobbed behind the Climackton goal, a phantom goal-keeper responding impotently to the scrabbling melee at the St Mungo end. Gregory, pale and gawky in his ill-fitting jersey, was much less active in the goalmouth proper; most of his movement was from the waist up and involved arm-waving and muscle-clenching. He was tired, having jogged bleary-eyed through the country park before breakfast that morning – an event which caused general consternation in his family, and particular worry to his father. He was also concentrating heavily on Dorothy. Lithe and darting, she was constantly in the heart of the action, exhorting or decrying the slow-footed Climacktonians, seething at bad moves or unfavourable referee's decisions, exulting when a tactic infrequently turned out right.

Gregory had never seen her look more splendid. Magic, he breathed to himself; she makes the whole game come alive. To Andy, he mumbled less effusively: 'Just watch the game . . . she's good, you know; she can move . . .'

'It's not right,' said Andy glumly. 'It's unnatural; it doesn't *look* nice.'

Gregory shook his head fiercely, still half lost in speech-less admiration. 'It's modern, Andy, it's good. Modern girls, modern boys . . . It's tremendous . . . look at her . . .'

Andy refused to be enlightened. 'Girls weren't meant to play football; it's too tough, too physical.'

'Tough!' Gregory allowed his attention to wander momentarily. 'Have you ever watched them play hockey? They're like wild animals. Even at twelve, thirteen, they'd kill you. Hockey was invented by Red Indians, you know,' he remembered, forgetting that Andy had been his original source of information. 'It was a form of torture. They used to make the cowboys play the squaws.'

'That was lacrosse, you moron,' rasped Andy. 'Anyway,

if women were meant to play football they'd be a different shape. How can you stop a ball and trap it in your chest with big – things hanging in front of you? Girls weren't designed for football.'

It was a point Gregory was unwilling to concede, but he was saved the effort by a sudden flurry of activity at the St Mungo goal. The goalkeeper had tried to clear a threatening ball with a long pass downfield, but Jeevons – Gregory's ex-striking partner – had deflected it by taking its full force on his left ankle. As his opposite number swooped to gain possession, Dorothy, gliding out of nowhere, trapped the ball, dribbled it past a defender and slammed it effortlessly into goal.

Shrieks of delight burst from Gregory and Andy; they clutched arms momentarily through the goal net.

'What a goal! What a girl!' Andy enthused.

Beaming, Gregory bunched jubilant fists and turned back to the field. At the far end pandemonium seemed to have broken out. The entire Climackton team were milling around a delighted Dorothy, planting kiss after kiss on her flushed and happy face.

'My God!' gaped Gregory, betrayed on all sides. 'Haven't they any shame?' Instantly the St Mungo players joined the melee; Dorothy disappeared beneath a universal tide of affection. 'Do you see that!' shrieked Gregory in outrage. 'My God! There are children watching this game.' He gestured impotently. 'This is what gives football a bad name!' The whistle blew, cancelling the orgy, to Gregory's huge relief. But the emotion proved short-lived. Within seconds the game was underway again. Whatever their personal feelings toward Dorothy, the St Mungo team were clearly desperate to redress the balance. A panting, fierce-eyed swarm thundered down the field towards Gregory.

'Watch the ball!' shouted Andy. 'Go out and meet it. Don't wait for it!'

Mild panic overtook Gregory, driving out all thoughts of jealousy. 'Watch the ball . . .' he mouthed, moving jerkily forward.

59

'Watch the winger!' Andy bawled, leaping up and down. 'He's coming up fast . . . wait for the cross!'

'Watch the ball . . . watch the winger.' Gregory was mumbling mechanically. Things were happening too quickly; he had only just worked out who the winger was. Keeping a sharp eye on him, he stepped out of goal. Instantly he was surrounded by a whirlwind of thrashing feet. The ball bounced behind him; a St Mungo striker skidded past and kicked. The ball cannoned into the back of the net as Andy mimed a perfect save from behind it. Glumly, Gregory collected the ball. He felt confused and oddly cheated; clearly his co-ordination was still giving him trouble. He'd have to work on that.

He felt worse when he found Dorothy waiting to take the ball. She snapped her fingers for it, too anxious to get the game started again to bother with recriminations. Gregory handed it over, feeling blank.

'I took my eye off it for a split second,' he said, rejoining Andy, shaking his head. 'Just two micro-seconds.'

'We need more women in this team,' said Andy fiercely. 'More new blood.'

'Aye,' said Gregory, watching Dorothy take up her position. He felt better now that she was safely distanced. 'She's some girl.'

Andy sniffed loudly.

The game had mildly depressed Gregory. True they had drawn – which was victory enough in itself these days – but, without Gregory's spot of bad luck at the goalmouth they might actually have won.

Not that he hadn't tried his very best. He was sure Dorothy must have seen that. She certainly hadn't snapped at him – quite justifiably – as she had at Jeevons and Pete and that McVicar idiot. On the other hand she hadn't exactly praised him either. Full of doubt, he stepped out of the shower, peeked to see if anyone else was around and then skipped across the tiles to where he had dropped his shorts against the wall. He hated being seen without his clothes on.

Perhaps, he thought damply as he eased on the shorts, the Galumphing Gourmet had been right. For all his inability to distinguish between Marilyn Monroe and a cream puff, Steve did have his head screwed on right. Perhaps he didn't stand a chance. No. He padded through to the dressing room, snatched up his towel from the bench and rubbed his head fiercely. He could understand how Steve could think that. Dorothy was so obviously superior, obviously glamorous, any podgy youth obsessed with food would feel outclassed. Gregory's situation was quite different; he didn't just fancy her, he felt for her, he *knew* her with all his being; in fact he loved her. No woman, however gorgeous, could ignore that.

Happier now, he dumped the towel, picked up his battery hair dryer and began drying his hair in front of a large wall mirror. He had, as usual, been the last to change. The dressing room was deserted. He liked that. It gave him more opportunity to dream about Dorothy in peace. The door to the corridor creaked open behind him. He had a glimpse of blonde, bouncing hair in the mirror and his mouth fell open.

'D'you have any plaster?' asked Dorothy, coming in and peering round. 'There's none in the girl's dressing room.'

'No! Uh... maybe... I'll get some...' Suddenly confronted by the object of his fantasies, Gregory's confusion was total. He went pink. He was instantly, horribly aware that he was wearing only his shorts. Putting down the dryer in a rush, he slapped a finger over each exposed nipple, realised the move was mildly insane, then snatched up his tee-shirt, squeezing it over his head, while endeavouring to keep an eye on Dorothy all at the same time.

She, meanwhile, oblivious to the consternation she was causing, plumped down on the bench beside Gregory's hold-all, and devoted her full attention to a small scratch on her knee.

'What's wrong? Does it hurt?' Gregory gabbled; to his intense relief he found a slightly grubby but unused elastoplast in the bottom of his hold-all. Handing it over, he sat down beside her.

'Don't panic; it's just a scratch,' said Dorothy mildly; she peeled off the plaster and applied it. 'I only wanted to save my tights getting blood on them. That big gorilla on the left wing – I got my own back, though – just before that last corner. I got my boot on his shin and scraped it right down.' She grinned at the memory. 'Big animal . . .'

Gregory raised uncertain eyebrows. He didn't mind Dorothy being tigerish, but deliberate brutality worried him a little. He took refuge in her wound. 'You'll have a bruise there.'

'Not if I let it bleed,' said Dorothy authoritatively. 'That's the idea. I don't bruise easily.'

'I do,' said Gregory. 'I bruise like a peach. *Boing!*' He thumped his chest in demonstration. 'Bruise . . . *Bop!*' Now his shoulder. 'Bruise . . . *Chung!*' He finished on a knee.

If this attempt at zaniness had impressed Dorothy she gave no sign; instead she bent to examine her other knee. 'See that? I was only three when that happened. On the beach. I was chasing a wee boy – I wasn't going to *hurt* him.' She said it almost in scorn. 'I fell on a bottle. That'll never go away. Marked for life . . . I'm imperfect!' She grinned, looking directly at Gregory for the first time.

His heart bumped; he beamed. 'It's nice, I like it,' he said.

'Really?' She smiled coyly – the self-satisfaction of her smile totally lost on Gregory who was only, blindingly, aware that she was being flirtatious. And with him! I'm on my way, he thought. It's happening; it's happening.

'I hurt my arm once,' he said. 'At the join. I can't get it any higher than this.' He lifted it to the level of his head. 'I used to be able to get it away up here.' He held it vertically.

'You just did,' said Dorothy flatly.

Gregory's face fell. 'No . . . it's the other arm.' He demonstrated, stretching out of his seat to show how useless the effort was. 'See? Stuck.'

They dissolved into laughter. A warm glow blossomed inside Gregory. It was as if they'd known each other for ages. As if they were boyfriend and girlfriend.

Dorothy leaned forward, lifting the collar of her football vest. There was a small white scar just below the nape of her neck. 'That was my big brother. I was only seven. He threw a bike at me. I can only see it in the mirror.' She ducked her head toward Gregory. 'It's quite nice, isn't it? A nice shape.'

'Mmm,' Gregory cooed. He was inches from her. He felt heady.

'Renaldo – that was a boy in Italy last summer –' Dorothy confided, rising. 'He said it was like a new moon . . . Very romantic . . . *La luna* . . .'

'*Ah si, si!*' The Mediterranean outburst stifled his sudden pang. He had a vision of sun-bronzed muscles, oily locks, a white-teethed Lothario brandishing ice-cream. '*Bella! Bella!*' he added, bravely.

'Ah, *parliamo italiano!*' Dorothy's eyes brightened. Since last summer Italian had become her private, conspiratorial language; she was taking it for 'O' level.

'No, not really,' replied Gregory disappointingly. 'Just "*bella, bella*".' He felt deflated.

'Oh,' Dorothy's interest waned. 'I think it's a wonderful language. So . . . alive . . . I want to live in Italy when I leave school.'

Gregory nodded glumly. This was even more serious. He'd thought of moving to Glasgow, or Edinburgh at the most.

'I can speaka da language,' Dorothy continued. 'I'm a quarter Italian and a quarter Irish on my mother's side.'

Gregory seized a receding initiative. 'I can speak Irish –' It was a passable stage brogue. Dorothy giggled quietly. Emboldened, he asked: 'What was Renaldo doing down there anyway?'

'Oh he lives there,' said Dorothy.

'I mean down there.' He indicated Dorothy's neck.

'Ah,' She nodded. 'He was putting some sun tan oil on for me.'

Olive fingers on her tender white back. The mental image was shockingly clear. '*Bella, bella,*' said Gregory softly. He felt awful. They fell into silence, both gazing at the rubber-tiled floor. 'Anything else to show me?' Gregory asked suddenly.

Dorothy looked at him blankly.

'Any major wounds when you were twelve? Fourteen?'

Understanding, Dorothy smiled. Gregory's emotional state improved. What could randy Renaldo do from several thousand miles away anyway?

'That's all for today, folks,' she said.

Gregory grinned. He was starting to glow again; all it needed was a little effort to keep this playful intimacy on the boil. He was just racking his brains when the door to the corridor crashed open with considerable force and a tall, fine-featured youth with coiffured hair burst in.

'Dorothy – there you are! Nice to see you!' he boomed, aiming straight for her. Behind him stumbled Eric, struggling to adjust his glasses and simultaneously keep secure hold of a large Pentax and flash unit.

'Good game?' thundered Gordon of the coiffure. He was the editor of *Bugle*, the school magazine, more commonly known as 'Bungle'. A sixth former, he was thought to have good university prospects; it was rumoured that his father – a local surveyor – had promised him a sports car if he got in. For that alone Gregory was prepared to loathe him.

Now – all hope of intimacy thrown out the window – Gregory leapt to his feet in outrage. 'Sorry – this is a dressing room, you can't come in here . . .' he flustered.

'You know Eric, don't you?' smiled Gordon, ignoring him. Dorothy returned the smile with obvious interest; she tugged daintily at her shorts as Gordon sat down in front of her. 'I'd like to have a chat with you,' he said. 'For the magazine – our summer edition, we're out just before the holidays. You can have a free copy of course –'

Dorothy's eyes widened; her smile blossomed. 'You want to interview *me*?'

'You bet,' Gordon enthused. 'We're covering two or three school personalities. We're doing you and that girl in the third year that had the triplets, and one or two others. You're pretty famous now, you know.'

Dorothy's smile became permanent. To Gregory's dismay, she seemed to be basking in the attention.

'Eric, pick off a few shots, will you?' Gordon snapped. 'Get the whole dressing room feel – and some nice big close shots of Dorothy.' He turned another dazzling smile on her. 'You don't mind if Eric uses the flash, do you?'

Gregory hovered awkwardly, his fists clenching and un-clenching. Smoothies like Gordon always had this effect on him.

'Eric,' he tried, drawing his friend aside, 'this is no place for a camera. People take their clothes off in here –'

Eric was fumbling with a light meter. 'Where better?' he whispered. His tone became more public. 'Could you move over here please? I want to isolate the lady in the shot . . . Keep well over here.'

Sighing, Gregory found himself shepherded into the shower entrance. Gordon had meanwhile produced a note-book and biro. 'I like to interview people like this,' he was telling Dorothy. 'No preparation, everything nice and natural – it's a theory of mine. Tell me, how are the boys taking it, your being in the team now?'

Gregory seized his chance. 'You guys are so predictable – always trying to make trouble,' he snapped. 'There are no problems at all, we're all very happy. Dorothy is a very good player. Everybody's very pleased.'

'Slow down, Gregory.' Gordon seemed almost hurt. 'This is an in-depth interview. I'm not a muck-raker. Dorothy?'

'Things are fine,' she said mildly. 'Some of them thought I wouldn't be heavy enough for the tackles, but I'm quicker than most boys. I can keep out of trouble. I take dancing lessons too, and that helps my moving.' Her smile became coy. 'What you've got to realise is that my body is quite – different.'

Gordon nodded in business-like fashion, his gaze drop-ping to take in her legs. 'I see what you're getting at. I'd like to talk to you some more about your body. You've got a good body – I would say it's one of your strong points. A real plus –'

65

Flash! went Eric's camera. For one dreadful moment Gregory thought they were going to ask her to take her clothes off.

'You must train a lot,' Gordon rattled on. 'Keep in shape – it must be very demanding. Do you have time for any other interest? What do you – and your body – do on Saturday nights for instance?'

'Saturday nights are special,' said Dorothy. She looked up as Eric flashed again. 'I like to do something special.'

'Right!' Gordon leaned forward. 'Saturday nights are for fun. Work hard, play hard. Exactly! Hey – how about doing something special this Saturday? We could go into town, have a drink or two. I could get to know you better – get the inside story maybe – we could have a really special time.'

Gregory went rigid. He was speechless, appalled by the youth's cheek, yet fascinated by his technique.

'That sounds like fun,' smiled Dorothy.

'You don't mind if I bring my notebook,' Gordon seemed determined to establish his credentials.

'No that's fine.' Dorothy was shaking her head, eager to please.

Flash! Flash! went Eric. Gregory's patience snapped. Watching Gordon try it on was one thing, watching him succeed was something entirely different. 'Come on! Can't a guy dry his hair and put his clothes on in here? This is a dressing room. You lot go and conduct your business somewhere else.' Gregory had been glaring at Gordon and Eric but, to his annoyance, Dorothy shot to her feet. 'It's really time I was changed.'

'We'll come with you,' burst in Gordon, pursuing her to the door.

'You're an interesting girl, you know. I want to find the real Dorothy . . . the one underneath the football strip . . . Dorothy the woman . . . OK?' He threw a sidelong glance past a bustling Eric. 'Cheerio Gregory.'

All three vanished into the corridor. As the door slammed shut, Gregory heard Gordon continue: 'Now about this Saturday in-depth thing . . .'

'*Arrivederci* Gordon!' Gregory snarled, snatching up his

hair dryer and smacking the on-switch. 'Hurry back!' He grunted and sniffed derisively.

'*Bella, bella,*' he muttered loudly. *Bella* Renaldo . . . *bella* Gordon . . .' His accent grew more exaggerated as he went on. He caught his reflection in the mirror, tossed his head and opened his eyes wide. 'I like to do thomething thpecial on Thaturday nighth –' he lisped. It was his worst day since he had fallen in love.

Chapter 7

Miss Ford looked up in surprise from her desk. She was a dark, sensible woman in her mid-forties. 'What's the sudden need to speak Italian, Gregory?' she asked.

'It's not sudden,' said Gregory emphatically. He was leaning on his elbows on the side of her desk, which meant, because of his height, he was almost bent double. 'I've been thinking about it for years,' he added, 'but it's taken a while to make up my mind.'

'It's very late in the term to start,' Miss Ford said doubtfully. As teacher of a minority subject she was always keen for new recruits – currently her class consisted almost exclusively of girls, like Carol McAndrew, Margo Crane and Dorothy Lennox. She wondered if Gregory's interest lay more in that direction.

'I've got some free time,' he said quickly. 'I could just sit in on any classes I can manage and catch up. It's very important. I want to live in Italy when I leave school.'

Miss Ford brightened. 'Ah you've been there, have you?'

'No...' Gregory's enthusiasm abated slightly. 'I've been to Ireland... and I met some Italians there, and they told me about it – in English. Renaldo could speak good English.'

'Renaldo? He's your Italian friend?'

'Not just him.' Gregory's face went blank; he appeared to be sweating mildly. 'There were girls there too. I just said him because he could speak English.'

Miss Ford pondered. Gregory's train of thought did not strike her as inordinately logical. She remembered him now from the third year – he was the boy who had described a French shoe shop – in apparently genuine ignorance – as a 'boutique'. French was Miss Ford's second subject. 'What kind of work do you want to do in Italy?' she asked.

'Well –' Gregory shrugged. 'I just wanted to learn the language and then see what there is going.'

68

'You should think about a course in technical Italian,' suggested Miss Ford.

Gregory hesitated. 'You mean words to do with engines and factories and garages and . . . work?' He made it sound like a dirty word. He had a sudden image of himself grubbing around a sun-scorched forecourt, pumping five-star into Renaldo's Ferrari Dino while Dorothy laughed brilliantly in the front passenger seat. 'I think I'd rather do the normal Italian and work my way down,' he decided.

Miss Ford smiled. Somehow she couldn't see Gregory as a star of her class. But she didn't want to squash his enthusiasm either. 'Well, we'll have to leave it just now,' she said. 'I'll have a word with your form teacher and see what we can come up with. I'm very pleased that you're interested, Gregory. It's a wonderful country.'

Gregory nodded madly. 'Wonderful language.' He straightened up. 'So – alive.'

'Did you pick any of it up at all?'

The question seemed to stump him. 'Only a couple of words –' He paused. Miss Ford's eyes widened expectantly. '*Bella* and . . . *bella*,' he finished lamely.

'Ah –' The teacher stifled a smile; she really shouldn't tease this way.

But Gregory was leaning forward again, a worried look on his face. 'Could you just give me something to be getting on with?' he asked.

'Yes of course,' said Miss Ford. 'What about *te lo dir'o?*'

'*Te lo – dir'o*?' Gregory tried.

Miss Ford nodded. 'It means, "I'll let you know", Gregory.'

'*Te lo dir'o*.' He rolled his tongue round the phrase. It had an attractive ring, a definite touch of romantic mediterranean evenings with *la luna* hanging in the background somewhere. The idea appealed to him. '*Te lo dir'o!*' he told Miss Ford, and backed out the classroom door.

Grinning and shaking her head, the Italian teacher turned back to her class notes.

Phil Menzies was worried. Worse than that, he didn't know why.

He stalked past the chemistry and physics laboratories,

the faintest hint of sulphur prickling his nostrils. Even stroking his moustache – now a thin but unmistakable bristle – gave him little comfort. Why should the headmaster ask him to 'pop in for a chat at three'? The atypically personal tone of the note didn't fool him at all. Phil distrusted authority even more than he distrusted the pupils – at least *they* couldn't sack him.

And his day had started so well, still bathed in the soft glow of yesterday's St Mungo draw – he had even, grudgingly, begun to accept the value of Dorothy. Was the headmaster going to congratulate him?

He grunted scornfully, and turned the corridor by the boys' toilets. No. Definitely not. That was never the way of Mr E.V. Twine, M.A. (Hull), commonly known as the Evil Swine. Blame was more his forte.

An appalling thought struck him. Could it be his order for a pair of Chuck Connors converse All-Stars (size 9) for the gym? Would the head believe that a pair of expensive American basketball boots, as used by the Harlem Globetrotters, were vital to the smooth running of the games department? He could always explain he was on his feet all day. Or worse –?

The record of Callas' and Gobbi's *Tosca* he had conned out of Grainger, the music teacher, on the pretext that it could be used to accompany rhythmic exercises in the gym –?

Phil gasped and stopped dead.

A rich operatic baritone had echoed down the empty corridor ahead of him. As he looked, Gregory Underwood appeared at a T-junction.

'*Te lo dir'o!*' he pronounced, gesturing theatrically, his chin tucked into his chest.

Without thinking, Phil darted into the shadowed side of the wall, found a door at his back and leaned into it.

A young woman teacher he knew only vaguely looked up from her desk.

'Sorry –' He became elaborately casual. 'I'm looking for Gregory Underwood – tall chap – fifth year?'

'This is 2A,' the woman said flatly.

Phil glanced round the edge of the floor. A roomful of

70

thirteen-year-old girls looked back at him in mild curiosity. 'Don't see him here,' Phil said. 'I'll push off. Thanks!' Red-faced, he ducked out. The corridor was empty again. Sighing, he padded back in the direction of the laboratories.

Gregory knocked at the door of the English class and ducked in shyly; he hadn't realised he'd spent so much time with Miss Ford. 'Sorry I'm late, Miss,' he apologized. 'I had to see Phil – Mr Menzies.'

Miss Welch looked disapprovingly over her glasses. She was a spare, pretty young woman with straight blonde hair. 'Sit down,' she said. 'I've just spent some time discussing the way illusion and reality are mixed together in *A Midsummer Night's Dream*. I won't repeat it for you. Perhaps one of your friends can fill you in later.'

Gregory made reassuring signs with his hands and picked out an empty desk just behind Steve, who wore the bored look habitual to him whenever the subject under discussion did not include cuisine – or possibly finance.

'Right, we'll go on with our reading of the play, starting at Act 3 Scene 2,' Miss Welch addressed the class. 'This, you'll remember, is Puck's speech to Oberon, the king of the fairies.'

Andy, hunched over his copy of the play, sniggered quietly at the reference.

'Perhaps –' Miss Welch's tone hardened '– you'd like to start where we left off last time, Andrew.'

Andy's face grew blank with dismay; public displays, let alone Shakespeare, did not appeal to him. He fumbled at the book. 'Er – *My Mistresss with a monster is in love.*

Near to her close and consecrated bower,
While she was in her dull and sleeping hour,
A crew of patches, rude mechanicals . . .'

His tone was leaden. Relieved, Gregory found the place in his own copy and immediately lost interest. Glancing round, he noted with surprise that Dorothy was in the class. His heart hiccuped. If he'd remembered he'd have left Miss Ford till later. She was sitting two rows away, near the

71

window, her eyes fixed on the text. She was wearing a new light blue blouse; it suited her, Gregory decided.

'. . . *An ass's nole I fixed on his head,*' Andy droned on. '*Anon . . .*'

There was a soft squeak at the window.

'. . . *this Thisbe must be answered,*
And forth my mimic comes. When they him spy –'

Two heads bobbed over the window ledge. There were further squeaks. A window cleaner's gondola rose jerkily into view. Inside were a grey-haired middle-aged man wearing overalls and a cap, and a youth in a boilersuit. They began to polish the glass almost daintily, as if anxious not to intrude.

'. . . *As wild geese that the creeping fowler eye,*' intoned Andy.

Peering through the glass, the younger window cleaner's eyes suddenly widened in recognition. He tapped the middle-aged man on the shoulder and began talking animatedly.

This, meanwhile, had attracted attention in the classroom. Looking up, Steve caught sight of the youth and began to wave enthusiastically. 'Miss,' he cried, 'There's Billy out there.'

'He "*Murder*!" *cries, and help from Athens calls,*' persisted Andy.

Miss Welch looked up and saw the figures at the window. Her face brightened. Billy – the younger window cleaner – had been a favourite in her third year classes. 'Hello Billy!' She left her desk and went to the window. 'Nice of you to drop in.'

Billy – a squat, pugnacious-looking boy with thick black hair – nodded and smiled at her behind the sealed glass.

'*I led them on in this distracted fear –*' said Andy.

'That's enough Andrew.' Miss Welch beckoned to a small safety window next to her desk. 'Come down here, Billy, so I can talk to you.'

Billy and his companion began to slide their gondola the length of the classroom.

'*And left sweet Pyramus –*' If Andy had heard the order to

72

stop, he was too hypnotised by his own monotone to register it.

'Andrew!' snapped Miss Welch, unclipping the safety window and opening it.

'... *translated there;*
When in that moment –'

Exasperated, Miss Welch scooped a paperback off her desk and tossed it at Andy. He looked up blinking. The class giggled. Miss Welch went back to her window as the gondola arrived. Both sides had to crouch down to reach the gap. 'You said you'd come back to see me,' she said brightly.

'Here I am,' Billy smiled. He turned to the older man squatting beside him. 'Can I introduce my boss? Miss Welch, this is Mr Wall. It's his own business.'

A disembodied and slightly damp hand appeared in the window gap. Miss Welch laughed and shook it. 'Pleased to meet you. How's our Billy shaping up?'

'He's a good lad,' Mr Wall replied enthusiastically. He seemed undecided whether to look at the teacher through the glass or guarantee audibility by tucking his head under the window gap. 'He's been telling me about all the characters in the school. He likes you. And he's told me all about *Julius Caesar* –'

Smiling, Miss Welch resolved his dilemma. 'I hope you're doing my windows for nothing, Billy,' she chided. 'For old times' sake?'

'Give me your glasses, Miss, and I'll do them too. No charge,' said Billy, squeezing down under the gap as Mr Wall moved back awkwardly.

Miss Welch took them off and handed them over. She watched as Billy gave them a brisk professional rub with his chamois. 'Thank you,' she said, retrieving them. 'And listen, why don't you come up and see me some time?'

Billy beamed delightedly. 'I will,' he promised. 'I'll use the stairs though.'

Miss Welch laughed again and, with a smiling wave, went back to her desk.

Gregory, in common with most of the class, thought how

73

attractive she looked when she smiled – some people were wasted on Shakespeare. As Mr Wall began to polish again, Gregory saw Billy mouthing 'See you at four o'clock outside' at Steve and gesturing two storeys down to the front of the school. Steve was nodding back. Until Billy had decided to leave school early that year, the two youths had been great friends. Gregory, seduced by the aura of bonhomie that had infected the class, found himself nodding too.

'Now,' said Miss Welch, breaking the spell, 'where were we Andrew?'

The Evil Swine leaned back in his plastic and metal executive swivel chair, steepled his fingers and gazed interrogatively at his MA certificate, which was displayed prominently in a brushed aluminium frame on the wall opposite the door to the school secretary's office. He was a large, barrel-chested man with a bullet head and thin sardonic lips. They made him look evil even when he was feeling quite benign. A black, full-length academic gown – of which he as inordinately proud – completed the satanic effect.

He lowered his head; his lips curled. 'Doughnuts?' he said.

Steve, sitting across the headmaster's teak-veneered desk, glanced at a notebook resting on his crossed knee. 'We're still doing two kinds, jam-filled and rings –'

The headmaster's eyes narrowed. 'What kind of jam?'

'What would you like?' countered Steve. He enjoyed the cut and thrust of the market place.

'Raspberry?' The headmaster spoke insidiously, as though making a particularly devastating debating point.

Steve smiled. 'No problem.'

The Headmaster nodded solemnly and resumed his meditation on past academic glories. 'OK,' he said eventually. 'Half a dozen.'

Steve scribbled quickly on his notepad. 'I'll throw in two ring doughnuts – usually some left on a Friday. Have you given the Petits Choux any more thought?'

The headmaster considered this. 'Tell me about them again –' he challenged.

'Well –' In his element, Steve waxed eloquent '– it's a basic choux pastry – I've got that perfect now, I've been working on it – and a parmesan cheese and egg mixture . . .'

He couldn't see how the headmaster could possibly deserve his nickname – Steve always enjoyed negotiating with him. And that was quite apart from the modest profit he made on catering for the school's increasingly popular Parent-Teacher Association teas.

Perhaps, thought Phil Menzies as he waited in the school secretary's empty office, it was his BSA dripping oil on the main playground again. That had been a source of special vexation for the Evil Swine ever since he had slipped in a particularly obvious patch while escorting the school governors on a tour of the premises; even worse than the abrupt loss of dignity had been the fact that a three-foot tear had appeared in his beloved gown. At least Phil had offered to pay for an invisible mender – while contriving never actually to admit guilt. He hadn't noticed any new tears in the gown lately. And his BSA hadn't dripped a spot since the weekend. On the other hand it had seized solid during a test run at lunchtime.

Voices approached the far side of the headmaster's door. Phil straightened on his chair.

The door opened. A grave-looking youth whose name Phil could not recall exited.

'And I want everything here in my office for three o'clock Friday. Is that absolutely clear, boy?' snapped the headmaster, standing behind him.

'Right, sir,' said the youth.

Phil nodded, rising as the boy eased past him. That was one thing you could say for the Evil Swine; he could put the fear of God into the rule-breakers.

The headmaster's head ducked past the doorpost. 'Mr Menzies – please come in.'

Phil followed him trying a placatory smile. 'Sorry I was a little early –'

The headmaster shut the door. Indicating the chair Steve had vacated, he sat behind his desk. Phil assumed an alert posture. The Evil Swine's face betrayed nothing; he could have been totting up his Pools results or planning a massacre that would have made Genghis Khan blanch. 'There's a girl in the football team,' he said.

Phil hesitated. This was worse than Pools or massacre; the cunning devil was trying to trap him with a personal opinion.

'Well . . . yes and no . . .'

'Yes and no . . .?' A narrowing of the eyes. Careful now.

'Yes.' He was about to tack on a tentative ' . . . and no' again when the headmaster became dangerously specific.

'What do you mean?'

'Well . . . we *could* have a girl in the team – if we wanted one.' Phil was squirming. He had a sudden vision of the Evil Swine chained in a goalmouth and bombarded with iron footballs.

'*Do* we want one?'

Phil sighed. As usual Lady Luck had crept up on him from an obscure angle, substituting a swift karate chop for the hoped-for kiss. He decided to be decisive. 'Well –' he said.

'I think it's a wonderful idea, absolutely splendid!' the headmaster interrupted. His face was instantly wreathed in smiles. It was as disconcerting as watching a contour map of the Sahara suddenly transform itself into the Himalayas.

'Yes!' Phil seized his chance. 'And she's a great wee player. Very fast in the forward line – she's not going to hold the team back one little bit – in fact –'

A raised finger stemmed the flow of gratitude. The Sahara momentarily returned. 'I see one possible problem area . .'

'Oh?' Phil swallowed.

The headmaster nodded solemnly. 'The showers. What happens about the showers?'

Phil glanced at the wall; the point of the question eluded him. 'She'll bring her own soap,' he said.

'And you'll undertake to keep everything – above board?'

The penny dropped and Phil almost laughed in surprise. He could just imagine how a little toughie like Dorothy would react to hanky-panky: if any of the weak-kneed lot in the team ever had the nerve to try. 'Oh no problem,' he stated emphatically. 'No problem there at all, headmaster.'

Chapter 8

At three thirty precisely a loud bell rang through the low modern building opposite the main gates of Climackton Comprehensive. Seconds later several hundred junior mixed infants spilled out into the roadway where gaggles of mothers and pre-school infants awaited them. Gregory, slumped over a desk by a second-floor window, caught the movement out of the corner of his eye and looked up with interest. His sister Madeleine had promised to wait for him. They were going shopping after school.

Sure enough two small figures detached themselves from the milling horde and crossed the roadway to the comprehensive's gates. One settled on a bollard and glanced up at the school.

Gregory raised a hand and waved his fingers. The tiny, seated figure waved back. Gregory smiled and resumed his mild interest in the class. He and Madeleine had been close for as long as he remembered. He wasn't sure if it was because of her quiet admiration for him, or his unforced tolerance of her. Either way they worked well together. It was no coincidence that Madeleine had been the first female Gregory had told about his Dorothy feelings.

'Can I walk you home, Maddie?' asked the second of the figures at the gate. It was a small, neat boy with expertly parted hair and all three buttons on his blazer buttoned up.

'Sorry, Richard,' said Madeleine. 'I'm kitting out Gregory tonight. He needs a new wardrobe for his affair.'

'Is it going well?' asked Richard.

'I think he's a bit shy with women his own age,' said Madeleine. 'I keep telling him he's lucky he doesn't have spots. That would put anyone off. He just needs to build his confidence.'

Richard nodded. 'Perhaps I can call round after tea. We

78

could go down to the country park and you could tell me how he's getting on.'

'OK but we might be going round to my auntie's.'

'That's all right.' Richard moved away. 'I'll see you, Maddie.'

Madeleine settled herself more comfortably on the bollard, though with no hint of slouching. In many ways she was a female counterpart of Richard, neat and unflustered with a faint edge of primness. Her face was round, her eyes cool and serious under a generous fringe. In a few years' time, if the mood took her, she might well decide to be pretty.

A battered Cortina with ladders strapped to a roof-rack shuddered to a halt at the next corner, and Billy the window cleaner climbed out. He had changed from his boiler suit into pale, newly-pressed slacks, a white jacket with wide lapels and a crisp, open-necked shirt. Waving a brief good-bye to the departing car, he strode across to the school gates, straightening his jacket with elaborate care. He glanced up at the school building, flexed his shoulders and settled against a bollard.

Madeleine ignored him.

Billy sniffed, lifted a new packet of Marlborough out of his jacket pocket and offered her one.

Madeleine shook her head, the gesture conveying with perfect economy her opinion of near-adults who unwisely attempted to foist adult activities on well brought up little girls.

There was a pause. 'Waiting for somebody?' said Billy.

Madeleine looked the other way. 'Yes,' she said.

Something of her disapproval filtered through to Billy. 'You're not giving much away. There are two thousand people in there.'

'I'm waiting for Gregory Underwood, fifth year,' said Madeleine.

'Gregory!' Billy's face brightened. 'Steve's pal – I know him. Are you Gregory's girl then?'

'I'm Madeleine,' she said. They lapsed into silence again.

The home-going bell in the comprehensive brought an

79

even more explosive result than in the junior school. As the main playground darkened with the exiting multitude, Madeleine and Billy picked out Gregory. He approached in a cluster composed of Steve, Andy and Charlie. They cried out and blew raspberries as they saw Billy in his finery. He grinned happily, delighted with the envy he'd aroused, and made an obvious display of the cigarette he was smoking. 'Hello children, busy day? Lots of homework?'

'Give us a smoke, big man!' Steve growled, bunching his fist in Billy's face.

Still smiling, Billy produced his Marlboroughs.

'Look at that!' gaped Andy. 'Twenty smokes in one packet! King size!'

Savouring his largesse, Billy handed round the packet. 'Parasites,' he said, 'living off the workers.'

'No thanks,' said Gregory. 'I'm in training.' He glanced sideways at Madeleine, more conscious that he should be setting an example than of any peril to his lungs. They hadn't greeted each other, but Madeleine understood; Gregory was self-conscious about women in front of his friends. She tagged along as they ambled away from the school.

'That was some fun with Miss Welch, eh?' Andy chuckled.

'Raquel?' Billy became blasé. 'It was a good laugh. She's a pure doll. She's fancied me for years. She's after my body. I might have to give in.' He flashed his eyes and smiled lasciviously. 'Why don't you come up and see me some time?' he cooed.

The others laughed. Steve leapt at him, eyes blazing, and began to take mock bites out of his arms and shoulders. 'Let me have you! I want you! I want to eat you alive –'

'Watch the jacket!' cried Billy, recoiling. 'I had to wet, wash and polish eighty-four windows to buy this!'

'Some job,' said Steve. 'Do you get danger money?'

'No,' said Billy, 'but if I die my mother gets her windows washed for nothing for twenty-five years, inside and out.' It was something Mr Wall had said and Billy was still unsure if it was a joke or not. The blank looks he got did not enlighten him.

They turned left into a pedestrian walkway between rows of houses. 'We saw something great last week,' said Andy. 'A nurse up at the annexe, through the window – an absolute doll!'

Gregory's heart jumped at the revelation. There were some things he couldn't admit even to Madeleine. He dropped behind slightly, unconsciously suggesting the 'we' did not include him.

'That's nothing,' said Billy. 'I can see incredible things fifty times a day through a window.'

Unease overcame Gregory's curiosity. He spotted an alleyway that cut off towards the shopping precinct.

'We're off this way. See you guys later,' he cried. 'See you Billy!' Shepherding Madeleine in front of him, he moved swiftly away.

'Bye bye Madeleine!' called Billy, stopping. 'If I don't see you through the week I'll see you through the window!'

With a last nervous smile, Gregory disappeared into the alleyway. Madeleine had not turned.

Billy sniffed. 'They grow up fast, don't they?' he said.

'Ten years old,' sighed Andy, 'with the body of a woman of thirteen.'

'Idiot!' grinned Steve, cuffing him.

Gregory found himself feeling peeved as well as uneasy as he and Madeleine crossed Flodden Way and entered the walk-way that led to the rear of the shopping precinct. Then he felt guilty about feeling peeved, and then he felt generally depressed because guilt and peevishness and unease *were* generally depressing.

He didn't dislike Billy – in fact they'd always got on rather well. He didn't really mind him boasting about his job and his new clothes – and even his exploits with the opposite sex. There was just an awkwardness that fell between people at school and people in the real world, even if the people outside were doing jobs of paralysing boredom. It was so easy, trotting to school every day, slumbering through classes, to pretend other things weren't going on beyond the main gates. Then, just when you didn't expect it, something jumped up and reminded you – like running into Gary that day on the motorway bridge – and you started to feel left out and panicky. Colditz feelings. It was then his mind leapt to Dorothy; if *he* felt so shut-off and childish, think how much worse it must look to someone as smart and glamorous as her. His heart wilted. A deep gloom approached, and would have swallowed him whole for a good part of the evening if Madeleine, after a long silence, hadn't suddenly perked up and began dispensing words of wisdom and cheer.

Trotting dutifully beside him she had thought he was mooning happily on Dorothy and needed to be quiet. Then, as his face drooped longer and longer, she realised something was amiss. She knew Gregory was going through a difficult time. She really wasn't looking forward to growing up herself – even if it did mean staying up for *Policewoman* and wearing a real bra. 'You need some new trousers,' she told him matter-of-factly as they slipped behind Woolworth's and emerged into the main thoroughfare of the precinct. It was bustling and crowded, late shoppers merging with idling homegoers. 'Those baggy ones are awful,' Madeleine grimaced. 'I'll see Mum about it. Blue ones would be nice — Italian. If you're going to start falling in love you'll have to start taking care of yourself . . .'

'Are Italians good dressers?' Gregory asked glumly; he was thinking of Renaldo.

'They have lots of style,' said Madeleine. 'And they make nice trousers.' She paused to glance in a shop window. Gregory waited. 'Richard's sister was telling me about Dorothy; she's very attractive,' Madeleine resumed. 'I *knew* you would fall for that type. She wears nice things; she's got style.'

'She's a quarter Italian,' said Gregory. His emotional state was improving marginally; if all these other people were taking such an apparent interest in his infatuation perhaps it wasn't such a dead loss after all.

82

'Don't get too serious about her, if you can help it,' Madeleine warned. 'Have you asked her out?'

Gregory shook his head; he still felt too leaden to go into lengthy excuses.

'I can help you,' Madeleine went on, 'I'm a girl. I can tell you things. You were good to me when other boys *hated* their sisters.' Gregory grinned faintly at that; it made him feel quite good inside. There really wasn't that much wrong with Madeleine. He started to think positively.

They paused again outside a menswear shop. It was having a sale of all wool sweaters. 'Which colour do you like?' asked Madeleine.

'The brown,' said Gregory unhesitatingly; he liked brown – dark colours seemed safe to him.

'Brown!' said Madeleine scornfully. 'That's you all over – grey, black, *brown*! You don't *think* about colours, do you?'

Gregory shrugged; he hadn't thought about it before. They moved on.

'If you don't take an interest in yourself, how can you expect other people to be interested in you? You've got to talk to Dorothy, you've got to ask her out. She won't say no, I bet you. But don't treat her too special. If you're too romantic it could scare a girl off.'

Gregory listened, rapt. Even if she was a bit young, it could be quite useful having a sister – a kind of mole in the opposition camp. 'What kind of things should I say?' he asked seriously.

'Good heavens!' exploded Madeleine, sounding at least thirty years older than she was. 'Don't plan it, don't *think* about it – *do* it!' She glanced down at his moccasins. 'You need new shoes too. And buy me a drink.'

They were outside a brightly lit cafe with tables that had yellow plastic tops and green tubular legs. They sat down next to the window.

'So I should think less about love and more about colours?' Gregory summarised.

'You've got it,' said Madeleine.

A waitress appeared behind her, and asked for their order.

83

'A ginger beer, please, with some vanilla ice-cream and some lime juice,' said Madeleine in one breath. 'But don't stir it *please*!' Suddenly she was ten years old again.

The waitress looked at Gregory.

'Coffee please,' he said.

'What colour?' asked the waitress.

Gregory glanced at Madeleine; it was clear he was under test. 'Brown please,' he said.

Madeleine sighed theatrically. The waitress went away.

'They don't do *blue* coffees here, Madeleine,' Gregory whispered. 'This isn't Italy. No style here at all.'

She stuck her tongue out at him. They relaxed and stared out of the window.

'Do you dream about her, when you're sleeping I mean?' Madeleine asked suddenly.

Gregory thought about it. 'Yes,' he decided.

Madeleine nodded. 'That means you love her. It's the one you have the dreams about that counts.'

The waitress returned and left the drinks.

'Who do you dream about?' Gregory asked.

'I just dream about ginger beer and ice-cream. I'm still a little girl, remember?' Madeleine chided. She was stirring her drink slowly with a straw, watching the colours mix. She smiled secretly. 'The nicest part is just before you taste it. My mouth goes all tingly.' She sighed. 'But that can't go on for ever.' And sucked fiercely on the straw. *That* was his problem, thought Gregory instantly. Anticipating the moment too much, relishing his own indecision. He must *act* – now while the iron was hot.

Chapter 9

'What did you mean,' said Gregory, sprawling on the living room sofa, '"no chance"?'

Steve, hunched three feet away astride a maroon leather pouffe, his eyes glued to the television screen, said: 'Eh?'

On the screen a woman in an apron was saying: '. . .One egg yolk if you want it that little bit smoother, and we can keep the egg white for the zabaglione later on . . .'

Gregory sighed loudly. Getting sense out of Steve during a cookery programme was like trying to discuss nuclear disarmament with a Celtic supporter during a Celtic-Rangers cup final. What made it worse was that this was the first opportunity he had had to discuss his Dorothy problem with Steve in days. After returning from the shops with Madeleine, she and Mrs Underwood had gone to investigate Aunt Morag's swollen ankles in Climackton Old Town. Mr Underwood was fitting in some evening lessons. Gregory had the house to himself.

'Look at that!' Steve said admiringly. 'You can tell a *real* cook by the way they crack an egg. Perfect!' He half-turned to Gregory, demonstrating the action with one hand. 'Only trouble is you don't need that egg, lady.'

Gregory got up and padded across the carpet to the tin of experimental marzipan almonds Steve had brought over for what he called 'test marketing.' Picking out the largest, Gregory asked: 'Do you know anything about Italians?'

'Excellent seafood in the north east,' Steve replied without shifting his eyes from the screen. 'Some of their regional pasta dishes are good too. Good with salads, very stylish all round . . .'

Gregory exploded. 'Food! Food! Food!' He stomped across the room, biting viciously into the marzipan. 'Is food all you think about? You're *unnatural*; you're a freak!'

Steve looked up more bewildered than hurt. 'You eat it,

don't you? I've never seen you turn your nose up at anything I've made –' The injustice of it sunk in. 'Hours and hours I've spent, making you lovely things. And all it means to you in the end is *food* . . .'

'Look pal,' glared Gregory, jumping on the sofa, 'I don't know whether you've noticed, but I'm going through a *crisis*.'

'Of course I've noticed,' Steve glared back. 'What do you want me to do? The whole world's got problems . . . you're just *obsessed* with a beautiful young *unattainable* girl, and you're at a tricky age anyway . . . so what?'

The counter-attack deflated Gregory. He said, sulkily: 'Stop saying things like that . . . unattainable . . . obsessed . . . This is love.'

'OK it's love,' said Steve, unimpressed. 'Go and attain her then. Amaze her with your suave charm and striking good looks. Oh, I forgot, you're the goalkeeper, *she's* the striker.'

Gregory gave him a sour look. With friends like Steve he was better off with spots.

'Look – in another ten years,' tried Steve, 'you'll look back on all this and cry your eyes out.'

Gregory drew his knees up under his chin and looked moodily at the floor.

'One key question,' said Steve. 'Have you actually talked to her, asked her for a date? Anything?'

Gregory shook his head.

'Well do it,' said Steve. '*Then* complain.'

Gregory looked at him. They were getting somewhere at last. Steve had come to the very same conclusion he'd reached three hours earlier which meant that it must be right. He uncurled on the sofa. 'If I get a date,' he said, 'can I borrow your white jacket?'

'No,' said Steve flatly.

The front door bell rang.

'Maybe that's her,' said Steve.

For a wild moment Gregory saw Dorothy, standing on the doorstep in shorts and football vest, holding a Telstar 5 and gazing up at him imploringly. Somehow the vision struck him as false. Then he saw Steve grinning at him and he went out into the hall and opened the door. There was no one there.

A polite cough drew his eyes down. Richard stood on the doorstep. He had changed out of his school uniform into neatly pressed corduroys and a belted leather jacket which was fully buttoned. He was also wearing a tie.

Gregory looked at him in disgust. He had a particular antipathy to male children over the age of five. *Neat* male children were even more loathsome.

'I wonder if Maddy's in?' said Richard.

'You mean Madeleine,' Gregory replied, glancing up the close. 'She's out with her mother.'

'That's a shame,' said Richard urbanely. 'I thought we could go for a walk. Maybe I could wait . . .'

'No,' said Gregory. 'They'll be ages.' He started to shut the door.

'Maybe she could phone me later on,' said Richard. 'She has my number.'

Gregory stared at him, appalled. Ten-year-old boys were bad enough, neat boys were worse, but neat *precocious* boys were an abomination. His feelings boiled over. 'Who are you anyway?' he snapped. 'You're talking about my sister; she doesn't go for walks with *anybody* – what's the idea coming to people's doors, seducing people's sisters – act your age – push off – go and break some windows, demolish a phone box. When I was your age –' He ran out of breath.

'You're Gregory, aren't you?' said Richard, quite unmoved. He reached out his hand. Unthinkingly, Gregory took it.

'Maddy's told me all about you. How are you feeling? Everything OK?'

Gregory gaped, his breath back; he snatched his hand away. 'There's nothing wrong with *me*. You're the one that should be worried – seducing children. You're heading for trouble – under-age walks, dates – you'll run out of vices before you're twelve. Push off!'

Richard accepted the outburst with equanimity, the air

87

of a rational man confronted with galloping insanity. 'OK Gregory, fair enough. Ask Maddy to call me anyway, if she wants. Richard's the name. See you around, Gregory –' He beat an orderly retreat to the gate.

'The name's Madeleine!' Gregory bellowed, leaning out of the door. 'Now push off!'

The USS *Enterprise* was in trouble. The warp drive had run out of dilithium crystals and the impulse engines were on the blink. Dr McCoy was sick, captain Kirk was in love again and Spock's ears were drooping – there were no stocks of a certain alcoholic beverage on board to revive them. Only Scottie could save the ship. Looping over a high snowy white mountain range, she hurtled towards a flower-strewn plain. At the last moment retro rockets fired, the keel gouged a deep furrow through the earth and the vessel came to a rest, leaning at a steep angle – broken, smoke-enshrouded, but safe. Then she blew up. Gregory tossed the Dinky toy model across the duvet, bored with the free-flowing fantasy.

He sat fully clothed against his bedhead, listened to the night sounds of the house. His father had stomped to bed fifteen minutes ago, Madeleine had just moaned quietly in her sleep next door; out in the close a randy tom was giving vent to his frustation. Gregory felt jaded but untired; as if the evening had ended too early. After such a concentrated bout of decision-making he wanted to get moving, to act, before some new Renaldo appeared on the scene – not to mention that inky-fingered smoothie, Gordon; he'd have to check up on that.

To think – he thought – even now Dorothy was curled up in her lonely bed somewhere on the other side of Climackton, her Adidas tracksuit no doubt draped over the bed-rail, a pyramid of Telstar 5s in the corner. He glowed, imagining her warmth beside him, and was immediately lost in a fond reverie. His eyes glazed. In a moment he smiled.

The tom outside whined again, closer now. Gregory's eyes re-focussed. With a shivery sigh, he rolled off the bed and moved to the window. Pushing the curtain aside, he tilted it further open. The night was black and balmy. He caught the will o'wisp flicker of motorway between the dark houses opposite.

'Miaoooow!' announced the tom below.

'Oooooommmmmiaooww!' echoed Gregory.

'Miaoow, miaow, miaooooooow!' whined the tom, rising an octave.

'Oooo miaow, miaow, miaooooooow, miaaaaaaaaaa!' Gregory screeched.

'Oh for pity's sake somebody fetch a bucket of water,' murmured Mr Underwood, two windows down, and turning over, went to sleep.

Three streets away, but on an equal level, dark-haired Susan, the girl with a fondness for ostriches, looked up at the odd sound which filtered through the open window of her bedroom. She was sitting up in bed, reading the nurse's scene from *Romeo and Juliet* and wondering why it was supposed to be so naughty. The caterwauling came again and made her grin. In an odd way it reminded her of Gregory.

The door was brown and locked; a Dymo tab under the room number read: 'Darkroom.' Inside an uncertain tenor bellowed: 'Just one Cornetto – geev it to meeee!'

Gregory knocked again, more loudly.

'Hold on,' shouted the voice. 'I'm developing!'

Gregory tapped his foot and looked up and down the corridor; it was nine-twenty-five and he was already late for the war of 1812 with Mr Stewart.

A bolt rattled on the door; it opened and Eric's tousled head popped out. He pushed his glasses more firmly onto his nose. 'What is it?'

'Can I come in?' said Gregory.

Frowning, Eric ushered him inside, closing the door quickly. He went straight to a table in the corner and lifted cloths off his developing trays. A small red light bulb shone dully from the ceiling.

'I'd make a lousy photographer,' said Gregory. 'I get scared in the dark.'

Eric grunted and made splashing sounds. 'What do you want?' he said.

'I just wondered,' said Gregory airily, 'how the snaps came out, the ones in the dressing room.' He was trying very hard to be nonchalant.

'Oh, Dorothy!' Eric brightened immediately; he gestured at the trays. 'I'm working on her now.' Gregory joined him. 'She's a beauty. She's a dream to photograph.'

'Really?' said Gregory coolly; he could only see a blank sheet in the bottom of one tray.

Eric was nodding fiercely. 'I could go for this girl in a big way. Look at that nose!' Slowly, like a very flat ghost, Dorothy's head and shoulders materialised in front of them.

Gregory's heart thumped; she looked gorgeous. 'Very pretty,' he said.

Eric fished the print out of the tray and dropped it into another beside it. 'Some of the guys reckon she's too much like a boy,' he reflected, 'but I think she's lovely.'

'Her like a boy?' Gregory allowed his enthusiasm to show. 'She's just modern.'

Eric lifted the print out of the second tray, shook it and clipped it to a wall rack; all the time he was nodding. 'You're exactly right!' he said. 'It's modern! It's the future! In another million years there'll just be people – no men, no women – just *people*. It's logical evolution. Evolution is the thing!' His glasses shone like dull red saucers.

Gregory looked at him doubtfully; it struck him there were limits to modernity. 'No more men or women?'

But Eric's notoriously rabid enthusiasms had been aroused. He began stabbing fingers at the Dorothy prints on display, making viewfinders with his hands and swerving round Gregory in search of new angles. 'This is a modern girl! Made to be photographed!' he raved. 'Boy, I'd love to get my wide angle lens on her . . . a low-key light . . . a hazy background . . . The face and body of the eighties! I could really *make* something of this girl.'

Gregory remained stony-faced; he had been through Eric's David Bailey mime before and he was none too happy about the interest he was taking in Dorothy's person.

Abruptly Eric calmed down, slipped a clean sheet into the printer and switched the machine on. 'One elephant, two elephant, three elephant, four elephant, five elephant . . .'

Gregory stared at him.

' . . .Six elephant. If you don't put the elephants in you don't get real seconds,' said Eric over his shoulder. 'Ten elephants . . .' He pulled out the sheet and snapped off the machine. 'Every print needs an exact exposure. This one needed ten elephants – I mean ten seconds.' Reassured, Gregory stood beside him as he dropped the print into the developing tray.

'Come on darling . . . nice and sharp,' Eric urged. Dorothy's smile took shape before them. 'Look how quickly Gordon moved in on her,' said Eric, suddenly. 'That guy knows exactly what he likes. I timed it in my head – one minute and fifty elephants and he had a date. That must be a record – even for him!'

That was not what Gregory wanted to hear; he had yet to discover how that situation was developing, nor was he in a mood to confess all to Eric. 'Yeah, what a guy!' he said breezily. 'A really fantastic mover, absolutely incredible. Absolutely!' He felt sick. 'Look,' he snapped, 'give us a photograph, will you?'

Eric glanced up at the sharp tone, then a tight, knowing smile spread over his face. 'Oh I get it . . . you fancy her too, eh?'

'No, it's for a friend, somebody really shy,' said Gregory, in no mood to quibble. 'Just give us the photo –'

Eric sucked in breath. He lifted the print and dropped it in the fixative, shaking his head slowly. 'This stuff's really expensive, you know; paper, chemicals, it does terrible things to your hands . . .'

Gregory, who had been about to snatch up the print, withdrew his fingers.

'Twenty pence,' he said.

'Forty,' said Eric.

'Twenty-five.'

Eric looked at him. 'I'll frame it for a pound.'

'I'll take it just the way it is, thanks,' said Gregory flatly.

Eric reached down a print off the wall rack. 'You'd better take a dry one. Don't want to drip all down the corridor, do we?' Financial deals over, he could concentrate on customer relations.

Happily, Gregory dug the money out of his trouser pocket, and handed it over. He took the print in return and rolled it carefully into a cylinder. 'Thanks pal.'

'Anytime.' Eric, having checked the money, grew effusive. 'Weddings... family groups... passports, sporting events...'

With a final wave Gregory cut short the advertisement by stepping outside. The corridor was quiet but, instinctively, he turned to the wall to slip the cylinder into an inside pocket. Content, he set off for his form room and the safe-keeping of his satchel.

Footsteps clattered behind him. As he turned the corner into the busy main thoroughfare leading down to the gym, someone tugged at his elbow. 'Are you Gregory?' It was a little, red-cheeked girl from the junior year; she couldn't have been much older than Madeleine.

'That's me sweetheart,' Gregory grinned. Junior girls made him feel comfortable. 'Who wants to know?'

'Dorothy wants to see you,' she said.

His confidence – and his comfortable grin – collapsed; suddenly his legs had turned to jelly; he was quaking. 'Dorothy?'

'That's what I said,' said the junior huffily. 'She'll be in room nine at breaktime. OK?'

Gregory did not notice her go. For a moment he was too shocked to be elated. Dorothy coming to *him?* Why? What could he have done wrong? On the other hand, perhaps the mere fact of his deciding to act had tipped some cosmic balance; perhaps his longings of the previous night had somehow winged themselves across town and roused her telepathically. Or he'd really upset her. She'd heard about his mooning and wanted to warn him off.

His brain was in a ferment. He looked at his watch. Quarter to ten. A whole hour to wait. His heart began to do little sprints and spurts.

Chapter 10

The break bell trilled. Gregory, who had been nodding at Miss Welch's views on *Pride and Prejudice* in an orgy of pretended concentration for the past ten minutes – first delighting and then deeply disturbing the young woman – sprang up and flew out of the door.

Room nine was on the top floor overlooking the front playground. He could reach there in about two minutes, but he didn't want to arrive red-faced and panting; four or five minutes' tardiness would indicate about the right amount of non-sycophantic enthusiasm. And there'd be no danger of him sweating. It also gave him time to slip into the toilets for a swift mirror inspection.

He chose a small gents just off the back stairs. It was empty but for a diminutive first former carefully washing his hands. Gregory gazed in the wall mirror two sinks along; there was a small spot on the right of his forehead but his hair hid that. He was glad he hadn't tried shaving again this morning; nothing looked worse than dried blood.

He wet his fingers under the cold tap and drew them slowly across his scalp, swearing silently at himself for losing so many combs. Then he noticed the first former fastidiously adjusting his parting. 'Lend us your comb, pal.'

'No,' said the junior, without turning.

Flummoxed, Gregory stared back at himself in the mirror. This was ridiculous. He had to be four minutes into break already. He stepped over to the junior, grasped him round the neck and snatched at the comb. The struggle lasted only a few seconds.

While the junior got up off the floor, Gregory combed his hair. 'Thank you very much,' he said, returning the comb and leaving. Worse than that little creep who was sniffing after Madeleine, he thought. Much to his annoyance, he was sweating slightly when he reached the top floor. Just before he got to room nine, he paused and took a deep breath. Then he glanced through the glass in the door. Dorothy was leaning against a desk, gazing into the room.

She looked marvellous. He was always surprised how many different and unexpected ways she could look so good.

He went in. 'Got your message, Dorothy,' he smiled.

Five girls looked up at him at once. Four of them sat on desks in a rough semi-circle in front of Dorothy. Gregory's expression wavered; he'd forgotten this was 5A's formroom.

'Oh hello,' said Dorothy; hers was the only returning smile, but it seemed quite genuine. 'I just wondered what you were getting up to at lunchtime.'

Gregory's drooping spirits revived. 'Nothing that can't wait a million years,' he offered.

'Good.' Dorothy's smile continued. 'Will you help me out with some goal practice?'

Gregory nodded enthusiastically. 'Yeah. Fine. Marvellous.'

'That's good,' said Dorothy. 'It'll speed things up. I want to practice shots at different angles.'

'I'll bring my compass,' Gregory said brightly; Dorothy nodded faintly. Gregory hovered. 'Well. See you at half twelve?' He was starting to glow.

'Fine.' She beamed; he felt the floor recede. 'Good. See you then.' Gregory backed towards the door, treading awkwardly like a grinning puppet; he raised a hand. It was all on again; they were moving forward. He floated out in a little bubble of happiness.

Dorothy turned to the other girls, her smile becoming wry. Margo, catching her look, raised derisive eyebrows; she began brushing Liz's long, chestnut tresses with practised, easy stokes. Carol looked out of the window. Only Susan, pulling her gaze away from the empty door, seemed less than bored.

Dorothy drifted towards the window, drawing Carol and Susan with her. Below them nearly a thousand young males milled in the boys' playground.

'Look at all these men,' said Carol.

'Boys,' corrected Dorothy.

'What's the difference!' broke in Margo behind them. Confident laughter filled the room.

It was on. No doubt. No question. Spring was sprung. Summer was icummen in. Gregory and Dorothy were like that. Like *that*. He crossed his fingers on the stairs, side-stepped to make way for a stumbling and incredulous male second former, and beamed seraphically at Miss Welch who happened to be crossing the second floor landing. She cast a single alarmed look in return and accelerated rapidly away in the opposite direction. She'd been warned about teenage boys developing strange obsessions when they started doing D. H. Lawrence for 'O' level but she'd been convinced Jane Austen was safe enough.

Gregory glanced down the corridor after her, and shrugged. He was in a mood to overlook any social oversight. As he watched, a gaunt and familiar figure stepped warily from the shadows and peered at Miss Welch's retreating rear. Lifting his eyes guiltily, yet totally unaware of Gregory, Phil Menzies coughed self-consciously, adjusted the whistle hanging round his neck and loped off in pursuit.

You old devil, thought Gregory, grinning. The whole school was throbbing with romance; ecstasy swam in the dusty air, and he was right there, in the mainstream, paddling away like mad.

He just had to talk to Steve.

Since this was Friday, the day after he had three hours unrestricted access to the domestic science laboratory – courtesy of the Evil Swine – Steve was extremely busy. He had two main retail outlets for his biscuits and buns: the senior cloakroom and the main boys' toilets on the ground floor. With summer coming on, he had recently begun to investigate a third, the cycle sheds in front of the main building. He was giving this serious thought when Gregory caught him up at the entrance to the toilets. Without warning he found his lapels grabbed, a breathless idiot grin swimming in front of him. 'I'm on my way, Steve; it's off the ground. Romance is in the air! Can I have your coat?'

'Hi pal,' said Steve affably. 'No.'

The idiot grin faded.

Steve pushed through the toilet door. Inside it was crowded. This was Steve's top-selling outlet, the school's alternative social centre; boys lounged against the cubicles, chatting and joking; one squatted on a cistern, laboriously manufacturing a roll-up; another thumbed absently through a Christmas edition of *Mayfair*; two more were shaking Coke bottles and spraying each other with foam; a transistor played punk. The place had something of the air of a speakeasy.

Steve sidled through proprietorally. He was pleased at the turn-out. If his new lines took off he couldn't help but clean up this week.

'I don't want to make a big thing over it,' hinted a voice behind him; Gregory was dogging his heels. 'But the coat would really help . . . it'd put the whole affair on a different footing . . . Just for one night, eh?'

Steve's mind had wandered. 'What are you raving about?'

'Me . . . Dorothy . . . date . . . coat . . . understand?' Gregory motioned patiently.

Steve stopped and looked at him. 'You've got the date, have you?'

'It's in the bag,' Gregory nodded. 'She's after me . . . I'm after her too, you know that, but she wants me to practise with her. This lunchtime.'

He was momentarily distracted by the sight of a cubicle plastered with Eric's prints. A junior sat on the seat behind a small card table and beneath a hand-scrawled sign that read: 'Our Dorothy; exclusive pin-ups. 10p'.

'My my, she wants you to practise with her,' cooed Steve. 'Well, well, it's better just to waste a lunchtime than ruin a whole evening. She's a very wise girl.'

Gregory glared at him. '*Football*. We're practising a game. I'm going to be in goal.'

'Not with my coat you won't,' said Steve moving on.

They came to the final cubicle, which was Steve's bakery outlet. The goods were displayed in trays balanced on the

96

cistern, across the toilet seat and on an upturned crate just inside the door. In charge was a short, wiry second-former with corkscrewing red hair.

'Morning, Kelvin my son,' Steve greeted him. 'How's tricks?'

'The coat's for later on! For the date!' snapped Gregory.

'The doughnuts are going like hot cakes, Steve,' explained Kelvin, 'but the marzipan almonds don't seem to be everybody's cup of tea.'

Steve threw a sour look round the busy toilet. 'Tasteless yobs . . .' he murmured, and picked up a small tin of change which was lying on top of the crate; he began to count the takings.

'Come on, Steve!' Gregory persisted. 'You gave it to Pete ages ago . . . why not me?'

'That's exactly why, Gregory old son,' Steve said, turning to him. 'Did you see the state of that coat the day after? Grass stains – beer stains – grease stains – . . .' He shook his head. 'Never again.' By way of compensation he reached for a doughnut and handed it to Gregory, who nibbled at it delicately; he had never been too keen on buying food in here.

'I'm not like Pete,' he said, only partially mollified. 'With Dorothy and me it'll be high-class – no stains, nothing like that . . .' He began to sound aggrieved.

Conscience pricked, Steve pocketed his takings. Then he saw a way out. 'I'll make a deal, old pal. You get the date, signed sealed and delivered, and then come and ask for the coat. Fair enough?'

Gregory's face brightened instantly. 'It's a deal. Thanks Steve. I really appreciate it. Would you like to throw in your brown shoes?'

Steve lifted his eyes ceilingward. 'I could use a persuasive berk like you in the organisation – you could help me off-load some marzipans onto an uncaring public; when are you going to start work for a living.'

Grinning, Gregory gave him a thumbs-up and backed away. He'd known he could rely on Steve; it was just a question of pressing the right buttons and, anyway, the gods were with him today. He could feel it in his bones.

Then he passed the cubicle selling Dorothy pin-ups and paused, frowning. The junior sales assistant blinked up at him through owlish glasses; he resembled a miniature Eric.

'I paid twenty-five pence for one of these,' said Gregory. 'How come you only charge ten?'

'Economy of scale,' said the junior in Eric's flat tones. 'You can have two for fifteen or three for twenty-five.'

'Then that's two you owe me,' concluded Gregory, snatching up a profile and a head and shoulders.

'Now hang on,' cried the mini-Eric. But Gregory had already gone.

Andy hovered by the water dispenser at the end of the long serving counter and juggled with his dinner tray as he surveyed the crowded school canteen.

It was, he'd told Charlie, a day of decision. It had come to him via a crumpled copy of *Cosmopolitan* he had found on a girl's saddle in the cycle sheds. Women, he'd read, often didn't realise they were attracted to someone until he'd made some kind of obvious advance. The implications of this had given Andy a sleepless night.

'Don't you realise, Charlie,' he'd explained. 'For every gorgeous girl who'll go berserk as soon as she sees you – and you know how many of *them* there are about – there are dozens, maybe hundreds of ordinary girls who'd really like you if you'd just give them the chance. By not going after them, we're denying them the opportunity of genuine happiness. It's our male duty not to hold back.'

Charlie had concurred, or at least he hadn't objected, which was about par for the course as far as he was concerned. Now they both stared dutifully around the long, low room.

Two rows of tables away Carol and Margo were eating together at a table for four. The other two places were empty.

Andy nodded in their direction; there was no point in overlooking the glamorous end of the market.

'Let's sweet-talk these two,' he suggested. He led the way over. 'Afternoon ladies – mind if we join you?'

Margo continued eating. Carol glanced up with a shrug, then went back to her meal. Andy positioned himself opposite her; he was aware his opening remark hadn't been dazzling, but at least he'd got some response from her. Charlie was forced to circle the table so that he could sit opposite a swiftly chewing Margo.

The boys set out their plates and began eating. Andy tried again. 'I'm particularly fond of lamb chops,' he told Carol brightly. His beaming smile went unacknowledged; fading, it caught Charlie's bland stare. 'Say something,' Andy mouthed. Charlie looked at his food.

There was another pause. 'How's the roast beef?'

Carol looked up dully. 'It's veal,' she said. 'It's OK.'

'Oh veal!' Andy seized his chance. 'Do you know what that is? It comes from little baby calves that they hang upside down. Then they let them bleed from the throat. Sometimes it takes ages for them to die. Isn't that interesting?'

Carol seemed to have grown pale. She put down her knife and fork. Margo swallowed and coughed. Andy's look of enthusiasm grew slowly more desperate; he glanced wildly at Charlie but he was gazing absently around the room. After a long pause Margo put down her knife and fork and the girls got up and left. Andy let go a long, despairing sigh and stabbed at his lamb.

'I tell you these women's magazines are a load of rubbish,' he said. 'It might be all very well in England or abroad.' He shoved a lump of meat into his mouth. 'We're in the wrong place.' He chewed savagely. 'I tell you where we should be – South America!' He took another bite, waiting for a reaction from Charlie. There was none. 'There's a town there –' said Andy, leaning across the table. 'Do you know what the ratio of women to men is?'

Charlie looked up at that.

'Eight to one – *eight* South American lovelies per one guy! That's the kind of place for us, eh?'

Charlie nodded, a smile creeping over his face.

'It's called Caracas,' said Andy triumphantly.

The ball skimmed over Gregory's left shoulder as he lunged awkwardly right and thumped into the back of the net.

Grinning, he converted the lunge into a series of apologetic and spastic gestures, including a shrug, a snapping of the fingers and a loud 'tccch!'

Dorothy waited patiently, apparently self-absorbed, at the penalty spot. She was wearing her Adidas boots, clean white shorts and a dark blue top. A picture of health and efficiency, thought Gregory, fumbling for the ball. He rather wished the shorts he had been forced to borrow, which now ballooned tutu-like about his waist, had been a little smaller, but Andy's pork-pie goalie's hat perched jauntily on his head, adding – Gregory considered – a certain rakish charm.

'This is great!' he enthused, rolling back the ball. 'I can really use the practice in goal.'

If Dorothy had heard, she made no sign. Lips pursing in concentration, she scooped the approaching ball with her right foot, turned and dribbled it in a fast, sweeping semi-circle.

Gregory watched the bob of her tight blonde curls, and began to bob restlessly himself. He was starting to feel uneasy about the seriousness of all this; for a girl who was after him, she seemed a little too distant to be playing hard to get. As he thought this he noticed the ball curving through the air towards the far side of the goal; he realised abruptly Dorothy had spun and shot in one smooth movement. Leaping across the goalmouth he felt satisfied the ball would never make it. Instantly it struck the goalpost, bounced past his shoulder and rolled into the back of the net. 'Great shot. You got me that time!' His enthusiasm was boundless. He picked up the ball and threw it back. Dorothy stood with her hands on her hips.

'Could you stop dancing around so much?' she called. 'It's very distracting.' Her left foot shot out, trapping the ball; she swept across the goalmouth to the opposite wing. 'How can you judge a shot dancing around like a . . .'

The ball flew from her feet, slamming past a nodding Gregory who had become suddenly statue-like. 'Great!

100

First class!' he beamed, unfreezing to return the ball. He shook his head in admiring disbelief.

'You're some player...' As Dorothy received the ball, her eyes narrowed mischievously.

'It's amazing,' Gregory continued to enthuse, 'I haven't touched the ball yet –' He spoke too soon. It hammered out of the blue, thudding into his stomach and doubling him up; he tumbled backwards and sat down heavily.

'Well held,' Dorothy grinned. 'You OK?'

Panting, Gregory struggled onto his knees; his smile looked as painful as it felt. 'Think I've broken my neck chain,' he said, glancing down at the ground; he began to fumble around in the scuffed dirt. This all seemed to be costing rather more than he'd anticipated. Finding the chain, he looked up to see Dorothy juggling expertly with the ball. She was totally serious again, mischief over.

'Come on,' she chided. 'We've only got another hour.'

Gregory climbed wearily to his feet. He wondered idly if Renaldo had gone through the same purgatory. Love, he decided, was really quite hard work.

Dorothy was jogging on the spot now. 'I want to try some shots on the move,' she said. 'Come out and tackle me, try and block, then move back and block some more. Use your feet – don't grab for the ball – and then –'

Gregory listened with growing dismay.

Andy glanced covertly at the pretty, dark-haired fifth-former sitting next to him. She was balanced on the waist-high top of the brick wall beside the boiler room entrance, legs swinging gently, eyes gazing boredly over the crowded rear playground as she munched an apple. Andy leaned nonchalantly against the brickwork and raised encouraging eyebrows at Charlie who stood dumbly by. This was promising, the look said. At least his opening remarks about the superiority of the Cox's orange pippin and the enormous pressures exerted inside the school boilers had not driven her away.

Carefully he adjusted a smile. 'Do you know,' he said confidentially, 'that when you sneeze –' The girl glanced at him warily – 'it comes out your nose at a hundred miles an hour?'

The fifth former gave a slow blink. 'Really,' she said.

Andy nodded eagerly. 'It's a well-known fact; imagine that –' He covered his nose and made an explosive noise. 'One hundred miles an hour!'

With a brief, withering look, Susan crunched loudly on her apple and slipped off the wall. Her eyes just topped Andy's head. She walked away.

Chapter 11

Gregory blinked the sweat out of his eyes. His face was purple, there were lead weights in his legs and malignant gnomes were pick-axing the backs of his knees. It was all he could do to keep a few paces behind a cool and serene Dorothy as they left the football pitch.

'Are you happy in goal?' she turned and asked mildly.

'S'OK,' Gregory panted. He lifted an arm to adjust his sliding headgear and found mud caking the length of his forearm.

'You could do with more control,' said Dorothy. 'You waste a lot of energy.'

'Tons left!' he insisted, and broke into a rapid jogging trot to make his point. His tutu-shorts sagged alarmingly. He stopped and hitched them up. He was starting to feel wretched and more than a little desperate. They'd hardly exchanged a dozen words over the past hour and all of them technical. The gym entrance was only yards away.

'Thanks for the practice,' said Dorothy. For the moment she looked almost sympathetic, and Gregory's hopes rose.

'No sweat,' he smiled. Then, glancing down at his muddy and dishevelled condition, picked up the joke before she could. 'Well, *lots* of sweat actually – but that's all right.'

Dorothy smiled tolerantly. 'Sorry you missed lunch.'

'Oh –' Gregory shrugged airily, 'lunch means nothing to me. Some fresh fruit, a few nuts . . .'

'Double apple pie and custard,' Dorothy added.

Gregory looked sheepish. 'That kind of thing,' he murmured.

They were at the touchline. The remnants of a smile played around Dorothy's lips. Then she glanced quickly at the school buildings. 'I'm off for a shower,' she said. And swiftly, without a backward look, she trotted off.

Stunned, Gregory watched her go. It took a few seconds

103

for him to realise what had occurred – a whole hour of physical agony and not once had he even hinted at a date. What had he thrown away? How could he have let it happen? He clenched his fists; knots of anger and self-loathing rose in his neck.

What had to happen to make him *act?* He took firm hold of his wayward shorts, and ran.

Dorothy was climbing the bottom step of the gym entrance when Gregory's shout made her turn. She paused as he skidded to a halt below her, his expression breathless but resolute.

'Just wanted to say,' he panted. 'Any time . . . for more practice . . . any time . . . just say the word.'

'Right, ta,' said Dorothy; she began to turn.

'Also –' Gregory's voice leapt an octave alarmingly '– would you like to come out with me?' There was terror in his eyes, but Dorothy simply nodded.

'OK.'

Gregory's mouth fell open; he blinked rapidly. Of all possible responses, he'd never dreamed this one. Perhaps she'd misheard.

'I mean on a kind of *date* –' he added disbelievingly.

Dorothy nodded again. 'I said OK.' Then she did turn and disappeared inside.

Gregory's mind went blank. After all this effort nothing should be this easy. There had to be some mistake. He flew through the entrance, catching up with Dorothy as she crossed the gym to the girls' changing room. 'Come on, stop fooling around –' He tried what he hoped was a disarming smile. 'I mean a real –'

Dorothy gave him a look of amused exasperation. 'If you're going to argue about it, forget it.'

'No!' The terror leapt back into his eyes. 'No, fine! . . . When?'

'Tonight. Half past seven under the big clock in the precinct,' said Dorothy easily.

A dim, bemused expression grew on Gregory's face. He nodded slowly. Dorothy granted him a swift, almost maternal smile and walked into the girls' changing room.

104

Gregory stood still a moment, only gradually realising that this vague, cotton-woolly kind of deadness he felt was in fact brilliant happiness. It also made him totally unaware that Phil had slipped into the gym at the far end of the room and witnessed the last exchange with deep suspicion, which deepened still further as Gregory let forth a sudden wild cackle, rubbed his hands together gleefully and skipped into the boys' changing room.

Frowning, the Human Dynamo loped across the floor, the Evil Swine's dire warnings rising to the surface of his mind. If that Underwood character was attempting to nobble his star player... He knocked at the door to the girls' changing room, pushed it open and leaned in. Dorothy sat on the low bench just inside, untying her laces. Steam curled from the shower room entrance at the other end of the room. 'Is that boy bothering you?' Phil asked gruffly.

'No.' The thought seemed to amuse the girl; she went on toying with her laces.

Phil grunted and looked glum. He'd almost screwed himself up for a confrontation with Gregory – one that would really settle matters; now he was depressed by an immediate sense of relief. He decided to cheer himself up. 'How's my favourite striker?' he said brightly, coming in.

'Fine,' said Dorothy. She was politely affable. Ever since that fateful day when she'd introduced herself, their relationship had been one of armed and uneasy neutrality; the armour was Dorothy's – she knew very well she could win any public battle. The unease was all Phil's.

'What do you think of the team?' he asked.

'I don't see too much of them,' replied Dorothy, glibly. 'I'm usually in front of them.'

Unaware of her irony, Phil nodded solemnly. 'That's the spirit.' He *was* aware that his own conversation was flagging.

Then Dorothy became more serious. 'It means a lot to me – being in the team.' It was a deliberate olive branch, offered as much out of self interest as kindness, but Phil grasped it gratefully.

'Oh me too – you've made more goals in two weeks than we've had all season.'

The ice was broken – they were communicating. Dorothy got quickly to her point. 'I was practising some turns on the ball,' she explained. 'I'm not too happy with them. I think I'm using my feet too much.'

Distantly halleluyahs echoed in Phil's skull as rank disbelief showed in his eyes. Not one grubby youth in a thousand would have perceived that a turn on the ball did not need acres of footwork. Yet Dorothy perceived it. A warm glow suffused Phil's face – though not before he had glanced warily about the room, convinced some malevolent fate would surely snatch this moment from him. At long, long last!

'That little remark tells me a lot about you, sweetheart,' he said in tones approaching reverence. 'You've got it. Here' – He tapped his temple – 'and here too.' He pressed a hand to his heart.

Dutifully Dorothy matched his gestures, as though following some new training exercise. For the first time she was giving Phil her full attention.

'And what,' said Phil, 'do you use to kill a ball's energy?'

Dorothy shook her head sharply.

In reply he pulled her to her feet, turned her round by the elbow and patted her bottom. 'This!' he announced triumphantly. 'Your gluteus maximus trap, my dear. This is what you do. You've got a high, fast ball – behind you.' He gestured dramatically to a point just below a distant light fitting, where shower room steam now billowed gently. 'You want to trap it, and turn. First you let the ball bounce – once. Kill that momentum. Then – and this is what foxes them – *reverse* up to the ball –' He crouched and began walking backwards. 'Catch it on the second bounce with your – fleshy part – drop down low with the ball –' He was almost squatting now, looking up at Dorothy. He paused for effect. 'You're right with it – OK, now up onto your feet – turn on your dead foot, and heel well out – remember, balance – and you're away!' He sprang up, grinning.

Dorothy nodded and smiled, clearly impressed. *'Jesu bambino!* That's really nifty!'

Phil bathed in the admiration for a moment, then, as embarrassment threatened, snapped back into the coaching role. 'OK, you do it now. I'll follow you through.'

He moved beside her as Dorothy went through the moves.

'Reverse,' he ordered. 'Down – trap – up – turn – heel out – balance – steady. And again: reverse – down – trap – up –'

She picked it up easily, whispering the words in time as Phil went smoothly from end to beginning again. In a minute they had speeded up, catching a steady yet relaxed rhythm that was indistinguishable from dance.

'We could call it the "Dorothy drop"!' Dorothy laughed.

Phil chuckled, lifting his arms with the rhythm. Steam from the unattended showers curled mistily about their feet. It reminded him of a Fred Astaire and Ginger Rogers movie he had seen on television the week before. As he danced on, it struck him – with a force few other things did – that suddenly, quite unexpectedly, he was feeling very happy.

Gregory's fractured tenor came to an abrupt halt; a mutilated verse of 'Dancing Cheek to Cheek' hovered in the air. He bent double in the bath, manoeuvring a thin sliver of his father's Imperial Leather in and out of his toes. He had forgotten to turn on the ventilator and the world had shrunk to a white, steamy globe the length of the bath. He launched into the chorus.

'Do your neck!' bawled a childish voice beyond the locked door. 'And under your arms!'

'Yeah, yeah,' Gregory muttered. 'Everything's under control.'

'Hurry up! You'll be late!'

He opened his mouth to protest, leaned out of the bath and scrabbled around on the carpet for his watch. Madeleine was waiting for him, pretending impatience and looking smug, as he padded pink and open-pored into his parents' bedroom, a ragged dressing gown wrapped tightly round him. He grinned at her delightedly, unable to hold it in, and plumped down on the chair she had prepared.

107

She picked up her mother's hair dryer and a plastic brush, switched on the machine and set to work on Gregory's towel-spiked hair. She was fussy and little-motherly and very content.

A worrying thought struck Gregory. 'Should I tell her some jokes?' he asked.

Madeleine pushed his head forward. 'Maybe.'

He grunted and pondered this for a while. 'Do you know any?'

Madeleine started to giggle. 'Don't tell her the one about Wonderwoman and the Invisible Man . . .'

Gregory caught her eye in the dressing table mirror, and began to chuckle too. Then, as he remember the joke more fully, he broke into a raucous laugh.

Madeleine continued to giggle politely, and punched Gregory lightly in the arm to make him sit still – and as a mild chastisement too; little girls, after all, were not supposed to appreciate that kind of humour. Gregory settled down, bottling his chuckles. He flashed a swift glance at the bed where Steve's grudgingly-lent jacket was laid out in its ice cream glory. Next to it was a pair of dark green Italian corduroys. From time to time the joke bubbled up in him again. He was feeling good, very very good indeed.

Chapter 12

He was feeling bad.

He stood before a low guard rail in a quiet corner at the enclosed end of the shopping precinct. Behind him, attached to a yellow tiled wall, loomed the big clock – actually the face of a gigantic Victorian station clock presented to the town on the demolition of a famous Glaswegian terminus. It was electrically powered now, and it read seven forty-five.

Outside beyond tall glass panes, seagulls fluttered in bright sunshine. They were the only sign of life. Gregory regarded them bleakly, and coughed. The doubts had begun the moment he had stepped out of Dumfries Close and the pampering aura of home had gone. Up St Mungo Way, through Glencoe Passage, into Flodden Way they had grown. The distance between the delicious anticipation of an act – and actually carrying it out – suddenly seemed an appalling gulf. By the time he had slipped down the side of Woolworth's, he had become a quivering wreck. How could he have *ever* thought a girl like Dorothy would take him seriously, let alone turn up on a date? Any normal fellow would have realised she'd been joking. Surely? For several yards he debated turning back and only his legs seemed to know what to do.

Then, passing the restaurant with yellow and green tables where he'd talked with Madeleine, his mood changed. First he decided he had to go through with it – he owed it to everyone, most of all himself; secondly, he wasn't that bad – not as smooth as Gordon with the coiffure and the promised sports car, admittedly, but certainly better than duffers like Andy or Eric or Pete, who was rumoured to have had his triumphs. Thirdly – and indisputably – he had the jacket.

It might be a shade over-wide at the shoulders and, to the cynical eye, rather more suited to a Mecca ballroom than a

109

deserted shopping precinct, but to Gregory it was impene-
trable armour; no right-thinking woman could possibly ignore
it, or think ill of the man inside it. This blaze of confidence had
lasted until he reached the clock – to find no sign of Dorothy.
He had stomped on his rising depression very swiftly then – he
was, after all, twenty minutes early. Since then he had boxed
the emotional compass a dozen times.

Idle chat would be OK – he'd already passed that test –
but how could he manoeuvre things onto a more sexual
footing? Should he take her hand at once, drape an arm
over her shoulder unobtrusively as they walked, or only try
to kiss her at the end of the evening? Then there was the
problem of the noses.

By seven-thirty he was a quivering wreck again. By
twenty-five to eight he'd persuaded himself girls were always late. By twenty to he was trying deep breathing exercises. At seven forty-six light footsteps echoed across the
precinct. Momentarily Gregory became frantic. His
father's borrowed after-shave suddenly seemed violently
excessive. He snapped to attention, framing an elaborately
casual smile, realised he'd have to hold it for too long, and
dropped his eyes to the information plate on the guard rail.
It struck him as a good compromise; unruffled surprise as
she appeared. The footsteps turned a corner behind him,
approached and stopped. Gregory lifted his head, his smile
already adjusted.

'Hi Gregory,' said Carol.

'Hello Carol!' Gregory breathed; his heart was too far
into its pre-Dorothy hammering to slow immediately.

Carol nodded and hovered; her hands were dug into the
pockets of a light raincoat. A large brown bag was slung
over her shoulder. 'Waiting for Dorothy?' she asked.

It was Gregory's turn to nod. 'Yes,' he said.

'She's not coming.'

The blow came too quickly for Gregory to react. He had
the sudden, slightly dotty feeling that he had gone deaf;
there were roaring silences on every side. All he was sure of
was that his casual smile was hardening into a bizarre
grimace. But he didn't trust himself to change it for any-

thing better. 'Oh – thanks.' He solved the grimace problem by sucking his teeth, shrugging and moving nonchalantly away to the sound of a halting, tuneless whistle. He found himself facing the locked glass doors of the Climackton Family Planning Clinic. 'Wrong way,' he murmured, grinning inanely at Carol. She waited for him to stroll back.

'Something turned up,' she elaborated. 'To do with her football, I think.'

Gregory's mouth opened and shut; his head bobbed.

Carol's eyes were raking his jacket. 'Is that Steve's coat?'

'No,' said Gregory emphatically. 'Steve's has a stain – right there.' He stabbed at the sleeve. 'See – no stain. Thanks for the word about Dorothy.'

Carol's gaze softened. 'S'OK. Couldn't leave you here all night.' She paused. 'What will you do now?'

It was a good question. Gregory blinked at her. Her look was speculative, even teasing. He had, after all, screwed himself up to a date; it would be daft to waste all that nervous energy.

'Fancy a walk?' he found himself saying.

'Where?' she asked.

Gregory hesitated: this was another aspect of his pre-Dorothy planning that could have done with more preparation; he hadn't really moved beyond the dancing cheek to cheek level. 'We could go up the sports centre,' he offered. He knew it sounded tame and the dismissive shake of Carol's head confirmed it.

'No . . .' She brightened. 'I'm pretty hungry, though.'

'We can go up Capaldi's. I'll buy you some chips.'

'Yeah – great!' her enthusiasm improved his emotional state instantly, until she added slyly, 'I was going up that way anyway.'

So it wasn't exactly Fred Astaire and Ginger Rogers, Gregory consoled himself as they started back the way Carol had come. Carol was shorter and squarer than Dorothy; her hair was the wrong colour – sort of dark and mousey – and not even her mother could accuse her of being a raving beauty. But at least it *was* a kind of date. If he had the misfortune to cross Steve's path, Carol would look feminine enough – at a distance; he could alway bluff later. For the moment he didn't feel up to working out his attitude to Dorothy.

They came out into the open area of the precinct. It was as deserted as the part by the clock. A solitary motor-cyclist pop-popped by on the road at the far end. Gregory wondered idly if it was Phil Menzies, prowling the streets of Climackton by night the way he haunted the school corridors by day. Because of this it was a moment before he realised he was alone.

'Gregory!' called Carol from behind him. 'Hold on a minute.'

Puzzled, he turned. Carol was standing in a telephone box, beckoning to him urgently. When he went back to her, she grabbed his shoulders, turned him round and made him stand with his back to the door. Now totally perplexed, he twisted his head to look inside. To his horror, Carol had lifted her coat and was peeling off her slacks. Frowning, she gestured to him to turn away.

Gregory flashed glances up and down the precinct. Had the girl gone mad? Was this some unsubtle ploy at seduction in broad daylight? He'd rather run a two minute mile, commit multiple murder than suffer any kind of public embarrassment. Then the door heaved open behind him.

'Ah that's better,' Carol sighed with deep satisfaction. 'I feel like a human being again.' Gregory gave a shocked squeak and took two steps backwards. He gaped at a magically transformed Carol. Gone were her slacks, her raincoat and her sensible school shoes; in their place were white winkle-picker stilettoes, black stretch tights, a skin-tight mini-skirt in broad black and white stripes, an even tighter scarlet top, deep purple lipstick and hair piled high in a punk-style explosion. He panicked.

'Look – I've got to go home. I really enjoyed the walk. You go that way –' He gestured vaguely down the precinct – 'I'll go this way. See you!' He had heard that Carol could be a little wild, but there was no way he would go down the road with this *freak*.

'Hold it, Gregory!' Carol checked him angrily. 'I thought we were going for chips.'

112

'Chips?' Gregory hesitated, as if dredging up a long forgotten memory. Suddenly inspired, he dug into his pockets. 'OK. Here's fifty pence. You'll get lots of chips for that. Bye!'

'Don't be stupid!' Stung now, Carol snatched at his arm, swinging him round. 'Come on – you're worse than my dad and he's old. At least he's got an excuse for being a twit!'

Gregory found himself being manhandled along the pavement. 'OK, OK.' He let himself be drawn; it was at least preferable to a stand-up shouting match. 'Just put your coat on,' he tried.

'Oh no.' Carol's grip did not relax. 'Come on, Gregory. All I'm asking for is a walk up to the chip shop. *I've* got a date. I'm going away. I've just got a feeling that something nice may happen up there. So *come on!*' The last emerged as an exasperated shriek.

'OK.' Gregory raised a mollifying hand. 'Just walk ahead.'

Carol sighed, transferring her grip to his hand. 'Gregory, hurry up,' she urged, increasing the pace. 'We haven't got all night!'

Why they should need any more time than the few seconds it took to say goodbye seemed a mystery to Gregory. Not even Steve would mistake this punk monstrosity for Dorothy. He shuffled in her wake, glancing warily from side to side.

Climackton's best known fish and chip shop – equally re-nowned for its pizzas and kebabs – was a cheery, glass-fronted edifice situated just off the main precinct in a mini-plaza of its own. A low curving wall at the foot of a grassy embankment occupied one side, incidentally pro-viding convenient seating for take-away customers. As a result the place was a minor social centre.

Gregory was annoyed to find it well attended this even-ing. He passed Andy and Charlie, both sitting on the wall and chomping lugubriously on a selection of chips, and gave a half apologetic, half embarrassed shrug as he fol-lowed Carol into the shop.

113

'Do you really fancy Dorothy?' she asked as they emerged a few minutes later. By the manner in which she was glancing up and down the plaza, it was not meant to be an invitation to soul-baring intimacy.

'Yeah,' said Gregory simply; he toyed with his chips. They found an empty spot on the wall.

'Can you drive?'

Gregory shook his head. 'No, but it runs in the family. Why?'

'It's just that Ricky Swift has a car,' said Carol. 'Dorothy knows him. He's up at the physical ed. college.'

She chomped noisily on a chip. It irritated Gregory almost as much as this new revelation.

'He must be quite old then,' he said drily. This evening was promising to be the worst of his life.

'Mmmmm!' Carol cooed with relish. 'He's nearly *nineteen –*'

That was it. Where charm or even impressive possessions scored, he reckoned he stood a fighting chance – but to be defeated by sheer *age*. 'Has he got any hair left?' he snapped. 'Ricky Swift! Sounds like something out of a comic. Does he wear a cape like Batman?' The image tickled his fancy; he began to chuckle. 'Quick Dorothy,' he intoned in a rich baritone. 'To the Rickmobile!'

'OK, calm down.' Carol looked away sourly. 'Don't get your knickers in a twist.' Her gaze seemed to catch on something across the plaza. Immediately she slid off the wall, plumping down her chip bag. 'Well, lover boy – time I was off.'

Gregory turned to her in surprise. Then he saw a pretty, blonde girl approaching; she was wearing a quilted anorak, a quiet floral skirt and a broad, knowing smile.

'Hey Margo,' called Carol. 'Here's Gregory. Dorothy stood him up so he's buying everybody chips and telling jokes.'

Gregory rose uneasily. He really didn't want his romantic misfortunes broadcast to the world at large. He was coming to the rapid conclusion that women were about as discreet in these matters as the average air raid siren.

114

'Have fun, Gregory,' said Carol; she grinned at Margo. 'Tell me all about it tomorrow. Oh by the way –' She bent down, extracted a pickled onion from Gregory's chip bag and tossed it aside. 'Pickled onions and dates don't mix. You might have to do some kissing later.' She smacked her lips together explosively. 'Bye now!' And with a dry chuckle, she tottered swiftly away.

Now thoroughly bewildered, Gregory stared after her. When he looked back, Margo was still smiling at him. He could think of nothing to say.

Margo took pity and patted his arm. 'I'll buy my own chips,' she said. 'You keep telling the jokes.' She eased past him towards the shop.

For a moment Gregory debated whether to follow her; somehow it seemed wrong to let your date order and pay for things by herself. But Margo wasn't his date – was she? At least she was prettier than Carol, and a lot more presentable – he wouldn't need dark glases to walk down the street with her. And she was blonde.

No clearer in his mind, he decided to compromise by wandering vaguely in the direction of the shop entrance – and found himself opposite Andy and Charlie.

'What's going on?' asked Andy.

Gregory shrugged. 'I'm not sure. I think Margo's after me. I get that feeling.'

A fiendish grin lit up Andy's features. 'It's a good night for it. Will you take her up the country park?'

Gregory shrugged again; he suspected that decision-making was going to be denied him tonight. 'I don't know. Do you think I should?'

'Aye!' breathed Andy; his tone implied limitless depravities only possible among bushes and open parkland.

Mildly reassured, Gregory nodded in agreement. Perhaps the evening's disasters could be redressed. He glanced at the shop and saw Margo standing by a pay phone near the back. She was replacing the receiver, a rather smug look on her face. What could that mean? A swift call to the parents warning them she might be late tonight? Gregory felt better by the minute.

115

She appeared at the shop door, a bag of chips in her hand, and beckoned him over.

Gregory winked at Andy and made a thumbs up sign. He strolled obliquely towards the shop, angling towards a walk-way that led to the main entrance of the country park. To his surprise Margo jerked her head the opposite way. Uncertainly, Gregory changed direction. He was beginning to feel misgivings again.

Andy and Charlie munched their chips and watched him trail Margo around the corner of the small parade of shops. Andy, too, was feeling far from secure. Seeing Gregory moon uselessly over Dorothy was one thing, watching him move from one friend of Dorothy's to another within the space of seconds smacked of an emotional injustice whose dimensions he did not care to contemplate. Instead he took refuge in philosophy. 'It's a fine evening for it,' he told Charlie, who grunted. 'There's definitely something in the air tonight. Something in the atmosphere.' His gaze lifted skywards. 'I reckon we stand a good chance of seeing a UFO.'

Gregory stared at Margo's dark heels clip-clopping a step in front of him and wondered for the third time whether or not he ought to take a lead. They had already crossed three streets at a cracking pace and the only personal contact so far had been Margo pressing her empty, and rather greasy, chip bag into Gregory's hand. He was beginning to suspect it was some kind of test – women, he'd read, could be very obtuse on points like that.

But then Margo seemed to sense his unease. She turned to him and grinned. 'Relax,' she urged.

'Where are we going?' he asked.

Her grin broadened. 'Relax.' She moved on. 'Enjoy it.'

'I am,' said Gregory. 'I will.'

At least she didn't seem disappointed. He kept pace with her now, exchanging tentative smiles. This was an even better sign. As they began to descend a walkway, he snaked an arm round her waist.

She stopped dead, glaring up at him. 'What are you up to?'

116

'Nothing!' He reddened, snatching his arm back. 'Nothing at all.' Then his bewilderment got the better of him and he became annoyed. 'Look – what's going on? Where are we going – where are you and I going?'

Margo's expression softened; she touched his arm. 'I told you to relax,' she chided gently. 'You can't enjoy yourself if you don't relax.'

Gregory sighed. 'I'm just a bit emotional tonight,' he said weakly.

'Well, that's OK. That's fine. There's nothing wrong with a bit of emotion. Come on now.'

Obediently, unable to shake the growing conviction that he was a lamb en route to some bizarre kind of slaughter, Gregory loped after Margo. One thing at least was certain: in all his sixteen years and two and a bit months he had never experienced an evening as strange as this before.

Susan leaned against a bollard halfway down Bannockburn Close and idly watched a middle-aged man wrestle with a Flymo lawnmower on his steeply-angled front lawn. Half a dozen lawns further along a middle-aged woman was having similar trouble with an identical machine. The lawnmowers buzzed fussily, mechanical gnats on the balmy, early evening air. Bannockburn Close was a private avenue of neat, cramped villa-style houses with front areas more noted for their stylish appearance than ease of mowing. It was also adjacent to the street where Susan lived, and even closer to the telephone box on her corner where she had received the news from Margo that Gregory was on his way.

She smiled at the deviousness of it all. The plan was working perfectly. She had had a good ten minutes to reach the rendezvous point, and a whole hour before that to put on her finery: dark, ankle-length skirt, pale blouse, navy blue blouson jacket with the pinched sleeves and – a crowning touch which satisfied her well-developed sense of style – a small black beret positioned securely on the back of her head. And that wasn't to forget the faintest touches of Revlon Creme Blush and Max Factor Hazy Blue, which had incidentally cost her a month's pocket money and three

117

nights' baby sitting a brute of a kid brother. If Gregory Underwood remained immune to all this he clearly wasn't worth the bother.

He was bound to be a little confused by the subterfuge, of course; he might even be annoyed, but that didn't worry her. Particularly dense ostriches could be amusing, or lovable, but never ever alarming. Even when they persistently over-looked the only half decent-looking girl in Climackton Comprehensive who cared more than a well-placed penalty kick for their attentions.

She snatched a glance at her wristwatch and looked up to see Margo turn the corner. A dazed but rather smart-looking Gregory was dogging her heels. Susan smiled involuntarily, then, as they drew nearer, straightened slightly.

Wrapped in his slowly turning thoughts, Gregory didn't notice the solitary figure at the bollard until they were within a few yards. Then he recognised Susan at once and was pleasantly surprised at how nice she looked out of school uniform; she'd hardly registered with him before, except as one of the Dorothy clique. It didn't take an enormous mental effort – nor the smirk that was now spreading across Margo's face – to figure out that he was due for another 'casual' encounter.

'Hello Gregory,' said Susan as they reached her. 'What are you up to?'

'Oh, we're just cruising,' Margo answered for him. She didn't seem in the least put out that Susan was focussing all her attention on Gregory.

'You're all dressed up,' she told him. 'Anywhere to go?'

Gregory looked warily from girl to girl; the air of gleeful intrigue was as thick as lentil soup, and much too heady for him. He puffed air into his cheeks, let it out slowly and shrugged.

'*I've* got somewhere to go,' Margo announced pointedly. 'See you tomorrow Susan.' She brushed past Gregory, reaching up to straighten his tie briefly. '*Relax,*' she whispered, grinned quietly and was gone.

Gregory glanced at Susan. The same grin seemed to have

118

settled on her. All this subtlety had completely unnerved him. He knew he was the object of some elaborate joke, but it was also a feminine joke and that made it doubly confusing. Whatever was happening, the night had long outrun his ability to cope.

Susan, however, seemed quite untroubled by his nervousness. 'I believe you're short of a date,' she said easily.

Gregory coughed. 'There was a bit of a mix up earlier. S'OK.' He nodded and tried to interest himself in the man with the lawnmower.

'Would you like to spend some time with me – on a kind of date?'

He looked at her. It was time to stop this bizarre merry-go-round. 'Look, I'm not really sure what's going on. Is this some kind of joke, all this with Carol and Margo –?'

Susan's smile widened.

'It's a joke, isn't it?' he asked.

She shook her head. 'Not a joke. It's just the way girls work. They help each other.'

Understanding dawned slowly on Gregory; he'd never been meant to meet Dorothy at all. This was the spot designated for him this evening – he'd been led to it, unwittingly, like a bull by the nose.

'You mean you and Dorothy –?' he began.

Susan nodded quickly; she preferred the spectre of Dorothy to be exorcised as soon as possible. 'Dorothy's a good sport,' she said emphatically. 'Anyway – how about you and me. What do you say?'

Gregory blinked at her; he could only manage a smile and a vague shrug. His first experience of the full force of feminine romantic machinations had quite overwhelmed him.

'Think about it,' Susan offered. She nodded to an adjacent bollard. 'Sit down over there and think about it.'

Meekly Gregory did as he was told. He really did need some time for his brain to stop flip-flopping. He couldn't decide whether he ought to be annoyed, or at least hurt, at being manoeuvred about so blatantly. On the other hand he was quite flattered to have a girl take all this trouble for a date. And a girl he'd hardly spoken a dozen words to before. This was clearly the right attitude to take. If he could have this effect without even speaking think how successful he'd be with some decent chat!

A little glow began to burn inside him. He sneaked a look at Susan; she was gazing nonchalantly but not unhappily up the road. She had a smaller face than Dorothy's – almost as nice, he decided, but different: sharper, finer somehow. Her legs were good to. The biggest mental adjustment was her dark hair; all the girls he dreamed about were blonde. This could play havoc with his fantasy life.

He took another, longer look. She was certainly well-dressed – obviously a woman of style. That was very important; he had very high standards. By now he knew he was quibbling: she was fanciable, she was friendly, and she actually appeared to like him. Miracles like this just didn't happen that often to a man Gregory's age.

He stood up and walked back to her, unable to suppress a rather foolish grin. 'OK – a kind of date,' he said. 'Can we start right away?'

Susan smiled and stood up briskly. 'Yes. We'll go to the country park. It's too nice an evening to sit in a bar.'

'Yeah – far to nice,' Gregory agreed eagerly. His heart was leaping. *The country park:* scene of lust, rapine and unfettered snogging – did she realise? They moved off down the close. 'What we'll do is just walk and talk,' Susan explained. 'We don't even have to talk that much either. We'll see how it goes.'

'Fine,' said Gregory; he grinned happily. Why weren't all girls this easy to get on with? It would make life so much simpler. It was at this point that he began to realise she was acting almost shyly with him – now that the protective shield of Carol and Margo had vanished; he started to feel more confident, more himself.

'I hope,' said Susan, glancing at him, 'you don't think I do this kind of thing all the time.'

'Oh no.' He shook his head dismissively; he really didn't want to think about rivals at the moment. A happier thought occurred. 'Can we whistle too?'

Susan considered this. 'Yes,' she decided, 'we can whistle too.'

Gregory began a halting, somewhat tuneless variation of *Walking on the Moon* by The Police. Uncertain of his musical direction, Susan contributed a random counterpoint. In a moment they were grinning at each other.

'If we were going for a drink,' asked Gregory, 'what would you have?'

'A Bacardi and coke,' Susan answered at once, 'with ice.'

'Same here.' Gregory nodded. 'With ice.' What a very positive girl, he thought. He decided he particularly liked positive women.

They rounded the corner of Bannockburn Close, mounted a walkway which led to a small wooden gate – a side entrance to the country park – and passed through onto a path of scrubbed earth beyond. It branched almost immediately, one track climbing a sparsely-wooded slope to a grassy hill above them, the other dipping towards a distant, oval boating lake. They took the hill path, and missed the two youths ambling towards the side entrance, one of whom took one glance at them, stopped dead and gaped.

'Do you see that, Charlie?' Andy gasped. 'There's definitely something in the air tonight – that's *three* women in a row he's had!'

Gregory was enjoying himself, he couldn't remember when he had last enjoyed himself so much. What pleased him most was how easily he could talk to Susan, and it was *talk*, not just chat; they were acting like good friends, except of course Susan was a lot prettier than Andy or Steve – and growing prettier by the minute. He found himself searching her small, bright face for flaws, just to convince himself he was mistaken.

'I like your jacket,' she told him. He grinned self-consciously; she appoved of his taste!

'I like your skirt.'

She ducked her head shyly. 'I like your shirt.' Now it was a game.

'I like your beret,' Gregory countered.

121

Susan beamed in genuine delight. She was very proud of her beret; a lot of boys wouldn't even have noticed it.

'Do you want to swap?' said Gregory. Susan laughed and handed it over. Her own fashion taste was vindicated; she could afford to be a little silly now.

Gregory settled it comfortably on the back of his head, juggling his head comically.

They reached the crest of the hill, passing a small tent which seemed hugely overpopulated; the sides bulged and flapped; giggles – masculine and feminine – issued from inside. Gregory raised shocked eyebrows; Susan giggled. Romantic urges seemed rife in the park tonight. Further on they found a dry spot beneath a ragged oak, one of the park's few old trees. They sat down.

'You know this is really good,' said Gregory, overcome with enthusiasm. 'I'm really enjoying myself.'

Susan nodded happily. 'I'm glad we bumped into each other.'

A bizzarre impulse overtook Gregory; he dropped flat on his back. 'Do you want to dance?' he asked. 'Don't laugh – it's really good. You just stretch out and listen to the music in your head. You can choose any tune you like. I'll start it off then you join in when you feel confident enough.'

Under Susan's amused gaze, he began to jiggle his hips, waving his arms and snapping his fingers in time with unheard melodies. She began to giggle, but in a moment she had straightened her jacket and joined him.

Gregory was feeling mildly inspired; it was not at all difficult with such a sympathetic audience. 'I'll tell you something,' he confided without breaking rhythm. 'And not a lot of people know this. We are clinging to the surface of this planet while it spins through space at a thousand miles an hour – held only by the mystery force called gravity!'

'Wow!' breathed Susan.

Gregory nodded. 'A lot of people panic when you tell them that, and they just fall off. But I see you're not falling off. That means you've got the hang of it – you've got –'

'Natural ability,' finished Susan, twisting her head to smile at him.

'Right!' said Gregory. Overhead the sky was mellowing.

After a moment, Susan paused. 'Why are boys obsessed with numbers?' she asked.

Gregory frowned. 'No, we're not.'

'You *are*!' Susan accused, laughing.

'Don't stop dancing,' Gregory warned, 'or you'll fall off.' He turned to grin at her, admiring the way her movements seem to fit in so well with his. It suddenly struck him that he could never imagine Dorothy being as quirky and amusing as this – not unless it involved some new training method. He realised, almost guiltily, that he hadn't given her a thought for at least an hour. Then, just as quickly, he forgot all about her.

Foot steps padded close over the grass. 'What are you two up to?'

They sat up abruptly. Eric loomed against the line of houses far below. He seemed a walking parody of the well-equipped photographer. Packets bulged from his pockets, an accessory bag hung from each shoulder; under one arm was a complicated tripod, under the other an enormous telephoto lens of bazooka-like proportions. Standing next to him, even more heavily laden, was his replica, the junior sales assistant from the boys' toilets. Both blinked owlishly.

'We're dancing,' said Gregory.

'Oh.' Eric's look was blank; his mind was clearly on deeper matters. 'I was just going down to the hospital annexe. To do the exposure test – for the flesh tone experiment.'

He glanced warily at Susan as he spoke, anxious not to disclose any details to her while still impressing Gregory that he might be missing the photograph of the century.

'Oh yeah,' said Gregory, understanding. 'The *flesh tone experiment* – of course. Have you got all the right gear?'

'Of course!' Eric patted his monstrous lens. 'Four hundred millimetres, this – opens up to one point eight, which with seven-hundred-foot candles at, say, a hundred yards, and film speed of three-hundred-and-sixty plus forced processing for another one point five stops –'

'Do you like numbers, Eric?' Susan asked.

123

'Numbers make the world go round,' he replied.

Gregory and Susan swapped grins, enjoying the intimacy of a private joke.

Gregory decided to elaborate on it. 'And how many – elephants – will you give it tonight?' he asked.

'Elephants!' giggled Susan, the nonsense of it all seemed to appeal to her.

'Well,' Eric considered, 'we can't have any time exposures. That would spoil the – image definition.'

'You don't want to spoil the – image definition,' Gregory agreed.

'Right. So that means a fast shutter. Say, at the outside, one-hundred-and-twenty-fifth of an elephant?'

'Sounds fine.'

Susan was giggling again.

'Coming then?' said Eric.

Gregory's smile faltered; he remembered that without tonight's extraordinary events he could well have been accompanying this expedition. 'No,' he said after a pause. 'But I'd be very interested in seeing the results.'

Eric shrugged his equipment more securely onto his shoulders. Mini-Eric, to one side, mirrored the movement exactly. 'Want to make an advance order for some eight by tens?'

'Put me down for six,' said Gregory as they turned away. He saw Susan laughing quietly. 'No,' he shouted after them, 'make it half a dozen!'

The photographic pair vanished in the gathering dusk. Gregory turned back to Susan. Behind her head a rosy glow spanned the horizon. They smiled at each other openly now, and Gregory felt his heart gently skip a beat. This wasn't dancing cheek to cheek, swanning through dream clouds with some impossible, unattainable woman. This was much warmer, more real, more exciting. He had the oddest feeling, gazing into her eyes, that he was somehow looking at himself. His head dropped and he moved next to her. They sat quietly, companionably, touching thighs.

'One more number,' Gregory said eventually.

'What's that?' Susan asked.

Gregory grinned apologetically. 'Eleven – got to be home by –'

'OK, Mister Spaceman.' Susan got to her feet. 'I'll walk you home.'

He jumped up beside her and they linked arms, easily, naturally, as if all the time and effort he'd spent planning how to get a girl into this particular intimacy had been a total waste.

The dust path was a grey snail trail in the dimness. Far off, lights began to spark in the straggling lines of houses, wink and flicker along the distant motorway. The night seemed to wrap Gregory in warm fingers, as tight and companionable as Susan's slim arm about his waist. It was as if all the windows in his head were open and a clean, fresh, intoxicating breeze were blowing through them. It made him voluble.

'I'm not so sure about this walking me home. What if the neighbours see me with a lady policeman. That could look bad . . .'

He saw the flash of Susan's white teeth in the darkness. She began to hum a tune, her feet skipping in a little dance of triumph.

'It's not really lady policeman. If that was the case real policemen would be men policeladies. Very complicated –' he burbled on.

'Be quiet and dance,' hissed Susan. She bumped hips, bullying him into a shared victory shuffle.

'Hey,' he said, 'you're a good little mover. Why is it that girls are so good at so many things?' He brightened. 'Bet I'm a better goalie than you –'

They clung in the porchway, just beyond the glass-filtered light from Gregory's hall, well within the balm of a new, swimming moon.

'That's better,' said Susan, surfacing. 'You've stopped kissing me like I was your auntie.'

She was wry, smiling, gently chiding in her moment of conquest since Gregory, now sporting a permanent and bemused grin, was clearly incapable of logical thought. He flashed a self-conscious glance into the darkness of the close.

'Nobody's watching,' she urged. 'Come on.'

They kissed again. Gregory felt his scalp lift fractionally. He wondered why he had ever worried about noses.

'Now what's my auntie going to say when I kiss *her* at Christmas?' he said eventually.

They beamed at each other, locked at the waist. Then touched lips again. Gregory narrowed his eyes. 'Three hundred and forty-two,' he announced solemnly. Susan raised an eyebrow, then smiled her understanding. If you were going out with boys who were obsessed with numbers kissing by them seemed only reasonable.

She stood on tiptoe to peck at him quickly. 'A million and nine.'

He hugged her for that, whispering as they parted again: 'How come you know all the good numbers . . .?'

She grinned delightedly.

'Thanks for seeing me home,' said Gregory. She kissed him.

'When can I see you again?' he asked, and kissed her.

'See you in history at ten-thirty,' she said. They kissed each other.

'That's a little early for me,' said Gregory. 'I'd like a date.'

They clung together for some time. Then Susan eased away.

'OK, Mister Spaceman. Twelve-thirty in room seventeen and we'll talk about it.'

Gregory nodded happily. 'Ten four.' He relished a last hug, perversely anxious to rush away and examine this extraordinary, rosily romantic glow that seemed to have enclosed and totally befuddled him. But it was Susan who lifted her head. She was – he decided finally – amazingly pretty.

'Goodnight Mister Spaceman.' She pecked him swiftly and affectionately on the cheek. Then she was gone. If Gregory's fear of being observed had prompted him to look up rather than round, the perfection of the last few moments might well have been marred. For at least five of them a small but steady trickle of bread crumbs had been descending from the window directly above the porch.

They came from a lemon curd sandwich which Madeleine had been chewing furtively – mainly because she had planned to stay awake to hear news of Gregory's date, and she would never have lasted without a snack, but also because she was intensely frustrated: the roof of the porch hid any direct view of the girl Gregory was talking to. Even climbing onto her bedside chair and stretching full length across the window sill made not the slightest bit of difference.

Now, as she heard Gregory's slow footsteps mount the stairs, enter the bathroom, and pad back towards his room, she stared fiercely at the door and willed him to pop his head round. But instead the light switch clicked next door, bedsprings creaked faintly and the click came again.

Infuriated, Madeleine flung back the bedclothes, skipped out of bed and tiptoed quickly out of the room. She cracked open Gregory's door, padded to his bedside and switched on his lamp.

Gregory lay on his back, fully clothed, his arms folded under his head; he was gazing at the ceiling, a broad, wondering grin on his face.

'How did it go?' she hissed eagerly, crawling on the bed beside him. 'Are you going to see her again?'

'Who?' said Gregory vaguely. 'Dorothy?' His grin seemed fixed.

'Who else?' whispered Madeleine, peeved.

'Well...' Gregory shrugged. 'Maybe... Susan, for instance...'

Angrily Madeleine seized him by the lapels of his jacket and began to bang his head on the pillow. 'Tell me – I'll hurt you – *tell* me!'

'OK, OK.' Still grinning, Gregory freed himself. 'Dorothy didn't show up. But I saw Carol and Margo and *then* Susan. She's lovely. We went in the park.' His grin broadened. 'I think she likes me. I'll see her tomorrow...'

'Did you kiss her?'

Gregory grew coy. 'No... maybe tomorrow.'

'You liar!' Madeleine bawled out loud. 'I heard you! You kissed about fifty times!'

Appalled Gregory sat up straight. 'Shush! You'll wake the mater and pater.'

Madeleine quietened down; she became more affectionate. 'I'd better kiss you too then.'

She pecked him quickly on the lips. 'It's hard work being in love, isn't it? Especially when you don't know which girl you love.'

Gregory nodded in solemn agreement.

Madeleine brightened. 'Who's going to be Gregory's girl . . .?'

Gregory made a face at her. 'You are!'

She whipped the pillow from under his head, plumped it over his face and thumped it lightly. Before he had pulled it away, she had jumped off the bed and skittered back to her own room.

Gregory settled the pillow back under his head and relaxed again, his idiot grin reassembling itself. Nothing of the evening seemed quite real yet. He wasn't sure if he felt that real himself.

And the biggest mystery of all was love. How *could* he have been so obsessed with a girl like Dorothy? She was pretty, yes, but so hard, so unyielding, so unsympathetic to him. Wanting her seemed incredible now. But even more unlikely was the fact that a few short hours with Susan could turn his feelings upside down. A girl he hardly knew. A girl he suddenly knew almost as well as himself.

He turned out the lamp and snuggled down, shaking his head in bemused wonderment. He closed his eyes but his grin wouldn't go away. Presently he gave a little chuckle.

Whatever mysteries of love – or football – existed, one fact alone shone like a beacon in a world of confusion: incredibly, improbably, Gregory Underwood was happy.